THE BOURGEOIS

THE BOURGEOIS

Between History and Literature

FRANCO MORETTI

VERSO

London • New York

First published by Verso 2013
© Franco Moretti 2013

1 3 5 7 9 10 8 6 4 2

Verso
UK: 6 Meard Street, London W1F 0EG
US: 20 Jay Street, Suite 1010, Brooklyn, NY 11201
www.versobooks.com

Verso is the imprint of New Left Books

ISBN-13: 978-1-78168-085-8

British Library Cataloguing in Publication Data
A catalogue record for this book is available from the British Library

Library of Congress Cataloging-in-Publication Data
Moretti, Franco, 1950–
The bourgeois : between literature and history / Franco Moretti.
pages cm
Includes index.
ISBN 978-1-78168-085-8 (hardback)
1. Middle class in literature. 2. Social values in literature. I. Title.
PN56.M535M67 2013
809'.93355–dc23
2013004072

Typeset in Fournier by Hewer Text UK Ltd, Edinburgh
Printed in the US by Maple Vail

to Perry Anderson and Paolo Flores d'Arcais

Contents

V.   Ibsen and the Spirit of Capitalism

Note on Sources

A few words on some sources used frequently in the book. The Google Books corpus is a collection of several million books that allows very simple searches. The Chadwyck-Healey database of nineteenth-century fiction collects 250 extremely well-curated British and Irish novels ranging from 1782 to 1903. The Literary Lab corpus includes about 3,500 nineteenth-century British, Irish and American novels.

I also often refer to dictionaries, indicating them in parenthesis, without further specifications: the OED is the Oxford English Dictionary, Robert and Littré are French, Grimm is German, and Battaglia Italian.

Introduction: Concepts and Contradictions

I. 'I AM A MEMBER OF THE BOURGEOIS CLASS'

The bourgeois . . . Not so long ago, this notion seemed indispensable to social analysis; these days, one might go years without hearing it mentioned. Capitalism is more powerful than ever, but its human embodiment seems to have vanished. 'I am a member of the bourgeois class, feel myself to be such, and have been brought up on its opinions and ideals', wrote Max Weber, in 1895.[1] Who could repeat these words today? Bourgeois 'opinions and ideals'—what *are* they?

The changed atmosphere is reflected in scholarly work. Simmel and Weber, Sombart and Schumpeter, all saw capitalism and the bourgeois—economy and anthropology—as two sides of the same coin. 'I know of no serious historical interpretation of this modern world of ours', wrote Immanuel Wallerstein a quarter-century ago, 'in which the concept of the bourgeoisie . . . is absent. And for good reason. It is hard to tell a story without its main protagonist.'[2] And yet, today, even those historians who most emphasize the role of

---

1 'Der Nationalstaat und die Volkswirtschaftspolitik', in *Gesammelte politische Schriften*, Tübingen 1971, p. 20.
2 Immanuel Wallerstein, 'The Bourgeois(ie) as Concept and Reality', *New Left Review* I/167 (January–February 1988), p. 98.

'opinions and ideals' in the take-off of capitalism—Meiksins Wood, de Vries, Appleby, Mokyr—have little or no interest in the figure of the bourgeois. 'In England there was capitalism', writes Meiksins Wood in *The Pristine Culture of Capitalism*, 'but it was not called into being by the bourgeoisie. In France there was a (more or less) triumphant bourgeoisie, but its revolutionary project had little to do with capitalism.' Or, finally: 'there is no necessary identification of *bourgeois* . . . with *capitalist*'.[3]

True, there is no necessary identification; but then, that is hardly the point. 'The origin of the bourgeois class and of its peculiarities', wrote Weber in *The Protestant Ethic*, is a process 'closely connected with that of the origin of the capitalistic organization of labour, *though not quite the same thing*.'[4] Closely connected, though not quite the same; this is the idea behind *The Bourgeois*: looking at the bourgeois and at his culture—for most of history, the bourgeois has definitely been a 'he'—as parts of a power structure with which they don't, however, simply coincide. But speaking of 'the' bourgeois, in the singular, is itself questionable. 'The big bourgeoisie could not formally separate itself from its inferiors', writes Hobsbawm in *The Age of Empire*: 'its structure had to be kept open to new entrants—that was the nature of its being'.[5] This permeability, adds Perry Anderson, sets the bourgeoisie apart

> from the nobility before it and the working class after it. For all the important differences within each of these contrasting classes, their

3   Ellen Meiksins Wood, *The Pristine Culture of Capitalism: A Historical Essay on Old Regimes and Modern States*, London 1992, p. 3; the second passage is from *The Origin of Capitalism: A Longer View*, London 2002 (1999), p. 63.
4   Max Weber, *The Protestant Ethic and the Spirit of Capitalism*, New York 1958 (1905), p. 24 (emphasis added).
5   Eric Hobsbawm, *The Age of Empire: 1875–1914*, New York 1989 (1987), p. 177.

homogeneity is structurally greater: the aristocracy was typically defined by a legal status combining civil titles and juridical privileges, while the working class is massively demarcated by the condition of manual labour. The bourgeoisie possesses no comparable internal unity as a social group.[6]

Porous borders, and weak internal cohesion: do these traits invalidate the very idea of the bourgeoisie as a class? For its greatest living historian, Jürgen Kocka, this is not necessarily so, provided we distinguish between what we could call the core of this concept and its external periphery. The latter has indeed been extremely variable, socially as well as historically; up to the late eighteenth century, it consisted mostly of 'the self-employed small businesspeople (artisans, retail merchants, innkeepers, and small proprietors)' of early urban Europe; a hundred years later, of a completely different population made of 'middle- and lower-ranking white collar employees and civil servants'.[7] But in the meantime, in the course of the nineteenth century, the syncretic figure of the 'propertied and educated bourgeoisie' had emerged across western Europe, providing a centre of gravity for the class as a whole, and strengthening its features as a possible new ruling class: a convergence that found expression in the German conceptual pair of *Besitzs-* and *Bildungsbürgertum*—bourgeoisie of property, and bourgeoisie of culture—or, more prosaically, in the British tax system placing profits (from capital) and fees (from professional services) impartially 'under the same heading'.[8]

---

6   Perry Anderson, 'The Notion of Bourgeois Revolution' (1976), in *English Questions*, London 1992, p. 122.

7   Jürgen Kocka, 'Middle Class and Authoritarian State: Toward a History of the German *Bürgertum* in the Nineteenth Century', in his *Industrial Culture and Bourgeois Society. Business, Labor, and Bureaucracy in Modern Germany*, New York/Oxford 1999, p. 193.

8   Hobsbawm, *Age of Empire*, p. 172.

The encounter of property and culture: Kocka's ideal-type will be mine, too, but with one significant difference. As a literary historian, I will focus less on the actual relationships between specific social groups—bankers and high civil servants, industrialists and doctors, and so on—than on the 'fit' between cultural forms and the new class realities: how a word like 'comfort' outlines the contours of legitimate bourgeois consumption, for instance; or how the tempo of story-telling adjusts itself to the new regularity of existence. The bourgeois, refracted through the prism of literature: such is the subject of *The Bourgeois*.

2. DISSONANCES

Bourgeois culture. *One* culture? 'Multicolored—*bunt*—... may serve for the class I have had under my microscope', writes Peter Gay in bringing to a close his five volumes on *The Bourgeois Experience.*[9] 'Economic self-interest, religious agendas, intellectual convictions, social competition, the proper place of women became political issues where bourgeois battled bourgeois', he adds in a later retrospective; divisions so acute 'that it is tempting to doubt that the bourgeoisie was a definable entity at all'.[10] For Gay, all these 'striking variations'[11] are the result of the nineteenth-century acceleration of social change, and are thus typical of the Victorian phase of bourgeois history.[12] But a much longer perspective is also possible on the antinomies of bourgeois culture. In an essay on the Sassetti chapel in Santa Trinita, which takes its cue from Machiavelli's portrait of Lorenzo in the *Istorie Fiorentine*—'if you

---

9   Peter Gay, *The Bourgeois Experience: Victoria to Freud. V. Pleasure Wars*, New York 1999 (1998), pp. 237–8.

10   Peter Gay, *Schnitzler's Century: The Making of Middle-Class Culture 1815–1914*, New York 2002, p. 5.

11   Peter Gay, *The Bourgeois Experience: Victoria to Freud. I. Education of the Senses*, Oxford 1984, p. 26.

12   Ibid., pp. 45ff.

compared his light and his grave side [*la vita leggera e la grave*], two distinct personalities could be identified within him, seemingly impossible to reconcile [*quasi con impossibile congiunzione congiunte*]'—Aby Warburg observed that

> the citizen of Medicean Florence united the wholly dissimilar characters of the idealist—whether medievally Christian, or romantically chivalrous, or classically neoplatonic—and the worldly, practical, pagan Etruscan merchant. Elemental yet harmonious in his vitality, this enigmatic creature joyfully accepted every psychic impulse as an extension of his mental range, to be developed and exploited at leisure.[13]

An enigmatic creature, idealistic and worldly. Writing of another bourgeois golden age, halfway between the Medici and the Victorians, Simon Schama muses on the 'peculiar coexistence' that allowed

> lay and clerical governors to live with what otherwise would have been an intolerably contradictory value system, a perennial combat between acquisitiveness and asceticism . . . The incorrigible habits of material self-indulgence, and the spur of risky venture that were ingrained into the Dutch commercial economy themselves prompted all those warning clucks and solemn judgments from the appointed guardians of the old orthodoxy . . . The peculiar coexistence of apparently opposite value systems . . . gave them room to maneuver between the sacred and profane as wants

---

13 'The Art of Portraiture and the Florentine Bourgeoisie' (1902), in Aby Warburg, *The Renewal of Pagan Antiquity*, Los Angeles 1999, p. 190–1, 218. A similar conjunction of opposites emerges from Warburg's pages on the donor portrait in 'Flemish Art and the Florentine Early Renaissance' (1902): 'the hands maintain the self-forgetful gesture of appealing for heavenly protection; but the gaze is directed, whether in reverie or in watchfulness, into the earthly distance' (p. 297).

or conscience commanded, without risking a brutal choice
between poverty or perdition.[14]

Material self-indulgence, and the old orthodoxy: Jan Steen's
'Burgher of Delft', who looks at us from the cover of Schama's
book (Figure 1): a heavy man, seated, in black, with his daughter's
silver-and-gold finery on one side, and a beggar's discoloured
clothes on the other. From Florence to Amsterdam, the frank vitality of those visages in Santa Trinita has been dimmed; the burgher
is cheerlessly pinned to his chair, as if dispirited by the 'moral pulling and pushing' (Schama again) of his predicament: spatially close
to his daughter, yet not looking at her; turned in the general direction of the woman, without actually addressing her; eyes downcast,
unfocused. What is to be done?

Machiavelli's 'impossible conjunction', Warburg's 'enigmatic creature', Schama's 'perennial combat': compared to these earlier
contradictions of bourgeois culture, the Victorian age appears for
what it really was: a time of *compromise*, much more than contrast.
Compromise is not uniformity, of course, and one may still see the
Victorians as somewhat 'multicoloured'; but the colours are left-
overs from the past, and are losing their brilliancy. Grey, not *bunt*,
is the flag that flies over the bourgeois century.

3. Bourgeoisie, middle class

'I find it hard to understand why the bourgeois dislikes to be called
by his name', writes Groethuysen in his great study, *Origines de
l'esprit bourgeois en France*: 'kings have been called kings, priests
priests, and knights knights; but the bourgeois likes to keep his

---

14   Simon Schama, *The Embarrassment of Riches*, California 1988, pp. 338,
371.

Figure 1

incognito'.[15] *Garder l'incognito*; and one thinks, inevitably, of that ubiquitous and elusive label: 'middle class'. Every concept 'establishes a particular horizon for potential experience and conceivable theory', writes Reinhart Koselleck,[16] and by choosing 'middle class'

15   Bernard Groethuysen, *Origines de l'esprit bourgeois en France. I: L'Eglise et la Bourgeoisie*, Paris 1927, p. vii.

16   Reinhart Koselleck, '*Begriffgeschichte* and Social History', in his *Futures*

over 'bourgeois' the English language has certainly created a very
distinctive horizon for social perception. But why? The bourgeois
came into being somewhere 'in the middle', yes—he 'was *not* a
peasant or serf, but he was also *not* a noble', as Wallerstein puts
it[17]—but that middlingness was precisely what he wished to overcome: born in 'the middle state' of early modern England, Robinson
Crusoe rejects his father's idea that it is 'the best state in the world',
and devotes his entire life to going beyond it. Why then settle on a
designation that returns this class to its indifferent beginnings,
rather than acknowledge its successes? What was at stake, in the
choice of 'middle class' over 'bourgeois'?

'Bourgeois' first appeared in eleventh-century French, as *burgeis*, to
indicate those residents of medieval towns (*bourgs*) who enjoyed the
legal right of being 'free and exempt from feudal jurisdiction'
(Robert). The juridical sense of the term—from which arose the
typically bourgeois idea of liberty as 'freedom from'—was then
joined, near the end of the seventeenth century, by an economic
meaning that referred, with the familiar string of negations, to
'someone who belonged neither to the clergy nor to the nobility,
did not work with his hands, and possessed independent means'
(Robert again). From that moment on, though chronology and

Past: On the Semantics of Historical Time, New York 2004 (1979), p. 86.

17   Wallerstein, 'Bourgeois(ie) as Concept and Reality', pp. 91–2. Behind
Wallerstein's double negation lies a more remote past, which was illuminated by
Emile Benveniste in the chapter 'An occupation without a name: commerce' of
the *Vocabulaire des institutions indo-européennes*. Briefly put, Benveniste's thesis is
that trade—one of the earliest forms of 'bourgeois' activity—was 'an occupation
which, at least in the beginning, did not correspond to any of the hallowed,
traditional activities', and that, as a consequence, it could only be defined by
negative terms like the Greek *askholia* and the Latin *negotium* (nec-otium, 'the
negation of otium'), or generic ones like the Greek *pragma*, the French *affaires*
('no more than a substantivation of the expression *à faire*'), or the English
adjective 'busy' (which 'produced the abstract noun *business*'). See Emile
Benveniste, *Indo-European Language and Society*, Miami 1973 (1969), p. 118.

semantics vary from country to country,[18] the word surfaces in all western European languages, from the Italian *borghese* to the Spanish *burgués*, Portuguese *burguês*, German *Bürger* and Dutch *burger*. In this group, the English 'bourgeois' stands out as the only case in which, instead of being assimilated by the morphology of the national language, the term has remained an unmistakable import from the French. And, indeed, 'a (French) citizen or free-man' is the OED's first definition of 'bourgeois' as a noun; 'of, or pertaining to the French middle class' is that of the adjective, promptly buttressed by a series of quotations referring to France, Italy and Germany. The female noun 'bourgeoise' is 'a Frenchwoman of the middle class', while 'bourgeoisie'—the first three entries mentioning France, continental Europe and Germany—is, consistently with the rest, 'the body of freemen of a French town; the French middle class; also extended to that of other countries'.

'Bourgeois', marked as un-English. In Dinah Craik's best-seller *John Halifax, Gentleman* (1856)—the fictional biography of a textile industrialist—the word appears only three times, always italicized as a sign of foreignness, and only used to belittle the idea ('I mean the lower orders, the *bourgeoisie*'), or express contempt ('What! A *bourgeois*—a tradesman?'). As for the other novelists of Craik's time, perfect silence; in the Chadwyck-Healey database—whose 250 novels add up to a somewhat expanded version of the nineteenth-century canon—'bourgeois' occurs exactly once between 1850 and 1860, whereas 'rich' occurs 4,600 times, 'wealthy' 613, and 'prosperous' 449. And if we broaden the investigation to the entire century—addressing it from the slightly different angle of the term's range of application, rather than its frequency—the 3,500

---

18   The trajectory of the German *Bürger*—'from (*Stadt-)Bürger* (burgher) around 1700 via (*Staats-)Bürger* (citizen) around 1800 to *Bürger* (bourgeois) as a non-proletarian around 1900'—is particularly striking: see Koselleck, '*Begriffgeschichte* and Social History', p. 82.

novels of the Stanford Literary Lab give the following results: the
adjective 'rich' is applied to 1,060 different nouns; 'wealthy', to 215;
'prosperous', to 156; and 'bourgeois', to 8: family, doctor, virtues,
air, virtue, affectation, playhouse, and, bizarrely, escutcheon.

Why this reluctance? In general, writes Kocka, bourgeois groups

> set themselves off from the old authorities, the privileged heredi-
> tary nobility, and absolute monarchy . . . From this line of thought
> the converse follows: To the extent that these frontlines were miss-
> ing or faded, talk of a *Bürgertum* that is at once comprehensive and
> delimited loses its substance in reality. This explains international
> differences: where the tradition of nobility was weak or absent (as
> in Switzerland and the United States), where a country's early
> de-feudalization and commercialization of agriculture gradually
> wore down the noble–bourgeois distinction and even urban–rural
> differences (as in England and Sweden), we find powerful factors
> counteracting the formation of a distinctive *Bürgertum* and discourse
> on *Bürgertum*.[19]

The lack of a clear 'frontline' for the discourse on *Bürgertum*: this
is what made the English language so indifferent to the word
'bourgeois'. Conversely, pressure was building behind 'middle
class' for the simple reason that many observers of early industrial Britain *wanted* a class in the middle. Manufacturing districts,
wrote James Mill in the *Essay on Government* (1824), were 'pecu-
liarly unhappy from a very great deficiency of middle rank, as
there the population almost wholly consists of rich manufactur-
ers and poor workmen'.[20] Rich and poor: 'there is no town in the
world', observed Canon Parkinson in his famous description of

---

19   Kocka, 'Middle Class and Authoritarian State', pp. 194–5.
20   James Mill, *An Essay on Government*, ed. Ernest Baker, Cambridge 1937
(1824), p. 73.

Manchester, echoed by many of his contemporaries, 'where the distance between the rich and the poor is so great, or the barrier between them so difficult to be crossed'.[21] As industrial growth was polarizing English society—'the whole of society must split into the two classes of *property owners* and propertyless *workers*', as the *Communist Manifesto* would starkly put it—the need for mediation became more acute, and a class in the middle seemed the only one that could 'sympathize' with the 'afflictions of poor workmen' (Mill again), while also 'guiding' them 'by their advice', and providing 'a good example to admire'.[22] They were 'the link which connects the upper and the lower orders', added Lord Brougham, who also described them—in a speech on the Reform Bill entitled 'Intelligence of the Middle Classes'—as 'the genuine depositaries of sober, rational, intelligent, and honest English feeling'.[23]

If the economy created the broad historical need for a class in the middle, politics added the decisive tactical twist. In the Google Books corpus, 'middle class', 'middle classes' and 'bourgeois' appear to have been more or less equally frequent between 1800 and 1825; but in the years immediately preceding the 1832 Reform Bill—when the relationship between social structure and political representation moves to the centre of public life—'middle class' and 'middle classes' become suddenly two or three times more frequent than 'bourgeois'. Possibly, because 'middle class' was a way to dismiss the bourgeoisie as an independent group, and instead look at it *from above*, entrusting it with a task of political

---

21   Richard Parkinson, *On the Present Condition of the Labouring Poor in Manchester; with Hints for Improving It*, London/Manchester 1841, p. 12.

22   Mill, *Essay on Government*, p. 73.

23   Henry Brougham, *Opinions of Lord Brougham on Politics, Theology, Law, Science, Education, Literature, &c. &c.: As Exhibited in His Parliamentary and Legal Speeches, and Miscellaneous Writings*, London 1837, pp. 314–15.

containment.[24] Then, once the baptism had occurred, and the new term had solidified, all sorts of consequences (and reversals) followed: though 'middle class' and 'bourgeois' indicated exactly the same social reality, for instance, they created around it very different associations: once placed 'in the middle', the bourgeoisie could appear as a group that was itself partly subaltern, and couldn't really be held responsible for the way of the world. And then, 'low', 'middle' and 'upper' formed a continuum where mobility was much easier to imagine than among incommensurable categories— 'classes'—like peasantry, proletariat, bourgeoisie, or nobility. And so, in the long run, the symbolic horizon created by 'middle class' worked extremely well for the English (and American) bourgeoisie: the initial defeat of 1832, which had made an 'independent bourgeois representation'[25] impossible, later shielded it from direct criticism, promoting a euphemistic version of social hierarchy. Groethuysen was right: *incognito* worked.

4. BETWEEN HISTORY AND LITERATURE

The bourgeois between history and literature. But in this book I limit myself to only a handful of the possible examples. I begin with

---

24   'The vital thing in the situation of 1830–2, so it seemed to Whig ministers, was to break the radical alliance by driving a wedge between the middle and the working classes', writes F. M. L. Thompson (*The Rise of Respectable Society: A Social History of Victorian Britain 1830–1900*, Harvard 1988, p. 16). This wedge placed below the middle class was compounded by the promise of an alliance above it: 'it is of the utmost importance', declared Lord Grey, 'to associate the middle with the higher orders of society'; while Drohr Wahrman—who has reconstructed the long debate on the middle class with exceptional lucidity— points out that Brougham's famous encomium also emphasized 'political responsibility . . . rather than intransigence; loyalty to the crown, rather than to the rights of the people; value as a bulwark against revolution, rather than against encroachments on liberty' (*Imagining the Middle Class: The Political Representation of Class in Britain, c. 1780–1840*, Cambridge 1995, pp. 308–9).

25   Perry Anderson, 'The Figures of Descent' (1987), in his *English Questions*, London 1992, p. 145.

the bourgeois before his *prise de pouvoir* ('A Working Master'): a dialogue between Defoe and Weber around a man alone on an island, dis-embedded from the rest of mankind; but a man who is beginning to see a pattern in his existence, and to find the right words to express it. In 'Serious Century', the island has become a half continent: the bourgeois has multiplied across western Europe, and extended his influence in many directions; it's the most 'aesthetic' moment of this history: narrative inventions, stylistic consistency, masterpieces—a great bourgeois literature, if ever there was one. 'Fog', on Victorian Britain, tells a different story: after decades of extraordinary successes, the bourgeois can no longer be simply 'himself'; his power over the rest of society—his 'hegemony'—is now on the agenda; and at this very moment, the bourgeois feels suddenly ashamed of himself; he has gained power, but lost his clarity of vision—his 'style'. It's the turning point of the book, and its moment of truth: the bourgeois reveals himself to be much better at exercising power within the economic sphere than at establishing a political presence and formulating a general culture. Afterwards, the sun begins to set on the bourgeois century: in the southern and eastern regions of 'National Malformations', one great figure after the other is crushed and ridiculed by the persistence of the old regime; while in the same years, from the tragic no man's land (more than 'Norway', certainly) of Ibsen's cycle comes the final, radical self-critique of bourgeois existence ('Ibsen and the spirit of capitalism').

For now, let this synopsis suffice; and let me only add a few words on the relationship between the study of literature and that of history *tout court*. What kind of history—what kind of *evidence* is that offered by literary works? Clearly, never a direct one: the mill-owner Thornton in *North and South* (1855), or the entrepreneur Wokulski in *The Doll* (1890), proves exactly nothing about the Manchester or Warsaw bourgeoisie. They belong to a parallel historical series—a sort of cultural double helix, where the spasms of capitalist modernization are matched and reshaped by literary form-giving. 'Every form is the resolution of a fundamental dissonance of existence', wrote the young Lukács of *Theory of the Novel*;[26] and if this is so, then literature is that strange universe where the resolutions are all perfectly preserved—they are, quite simply, the texts we still read—while the dissonances have quietly vanished from sight: the more thoroughly, the more successful their resolution turned out to be.

There is something ghostly, in this history where questions disappear, and answers survive. But if we accept the idea of literary form as the fossil remains of what had once been a living and problematic present; and if we work our way backwards, 'reverse-engineering' it to understand the problem it was designed to solve; if we do this, then formal analysis may unlock—in principle, if not always in practice—a dimension of the past that would otherwise remain hidden. Here lies its possible contribution to historical knowledge: by understanding the opacity of Ibsen's hints to the past, or the oblique semantics of Victorian adjectives, or even (at first sight, not a cheerful task) the role of the gerund in *Robinson Crusoe*, we enter a realm of shadows, where the past recovers its voice, and still speaks to us.[27]

---

26 Georg Lukács, *The Theory of the Novel*, Cambridge, MA, 1974 (1914–15), p. 62.

27 Aesthetic forms as structured responses to social contradictions: given this relationship between literary and social history, I assumed that the essay 'Serious Century', though originally written for a literary collection, would fit quite smoothly into this book (after all, its working title had long been 'On Bourgeois Seriousness'). But when I re-read the essay, I immediately felt (and I mean *felt*: irrationally, and irresistibly) that I had to cut much of the original, and reformulate the rest. The editing done, I realized that it mostly concerned three sections—all entitled 'Parting of the Ways' in the original version—that had outlined the wider morphospace within which the forms of bourgeois seriousness had taken shape. What I felt the need to eliminate, in other words, was the spectrum of formal variations that had been historically available; what survives is the result of the nineteenth-century selection process. In a book on bourgeois

5. ABSTRACT HERO

But speaks to us, *only* through the medium of form. Stories, and styles: that's where I found the bourgeois. Styles, especially; which came as quite a surprise, considering how often narratives are viewed as the foundations of social identity,[28] and how frequently the bourgeoisie has been identified with turbulence and change—from some famous scenes of the *Phenomenology*, to the *Manifesto*'s 'all that is solid melts into air', and Schumpeter's creative destruction. So, I expected bourgeois literature to be defined by new and unpredictable plots: 'leaps into the dark', as Elster writes of capitalist innovations.[29] And instead, as I argue in 'Serious Century', the opposite seems to have been the case: *regularity*, not disequilibrium, was the great narrative invention of bourgeois Europe.[30] All that was solid, became more so.

---

culture, this seems like a plausible choice; but it highlights the difference between literary history as history *of literature*—where the plurality, and even randomness, of formal options is a key aspect of the picture—and literary history as (part of the) history *of society*: where what matters is instead the connection between a specific form and its social function.

28   A recent instance, from a book on the French bourgeoisie: 'I posit here that the existence of social groups, while rooted in the material world, is shaped by language, and more specifically by narrative: in order for a group to claim a role as an actor in society and polity, it must have a story or stories about itself.' Sarah Maza, *The Myth of the French Bourgeoisie: An Essay on the Social Imaginary, 1750–1850*, Cambridge, MA, 2003, p. 6.

29   Schumpeter 'praised capitalism not because of its efficiency and rationality, but because of its dynamic character . . . Rather than gloss over the creative and unpredictable aspects of innovation, he made these into the cornerstone of his theory. Innovation is essentially a disequilibrium phenomenon—a leap into the dark.' Jon Elster, *Explaining Technical Change: A Case Study in the Philosophy of Science*, Cambridge 1983, pp. 11, 112.

30   The same bourgeois resistance to narrative emerges from Richard Helgerson's study of Dutch Golden Age realism: a visual culture where 'women, children, servants, peasants, craftsmen and interloping male suitors *act*', whereas 'upper class male householders . . . *are*', and tend to find their form of choice in the non-narrative genre of the portrait. See 'Soldiers and Enigmatic Girls: The

Why? The main reason lies probably in the bourgeois himself. In the course of the nineteenth century, once the stigma against 'new wealth' had been overcome, a few recurrent traits clustered around this figure: energy, first of all; self-restraint; intellectual clarity; commercial honesty; a strong sense of goals. All 'good' traits; but not good enough to match the type of narrative hero—warrior, knight, conqueror, adventurer—on whom Western story-telling had relied for, literally, millennia. 'The stock exchange is a poor substitute for the Holy Grail', wrote Schumpeter, mockingly; and business life— 'in the office, among columns of figures'—is doomed to be 'essentially unheroic'.[31] It's a major discontinuity between the old and the new ruling class: whereas the aristocracy had shamelessly idealized itself in a whole gallery of intrepid knights, the bourgeoisie produced no such myth of itself. The great mechanism of adventure was being eroded by bourgeois civilization—and without adventure, characters lost the stamp of *uniqueness* that comes from the encounter with the unknown.[32] Compared to a knight, a bourgeois appears un-marked and elusive; similar to any other bourgeois. Here is a scene from the beginning of *North and South*, where the heroine describes a Manchester industrialist to her mother:

> 'Oh! I hardly know what he is like', said Margaret . . . 'About thirty, with a face that is neither exactly plain, nor yet handsome, nothing remarkable—not quite a gentleman; but that was hardly to be expected.'

Politics of Dutch Domestic Realism, 1650–1672', *Representations* 58 (1997), p. 55.

31   Joseph A. Schumpeter, *Capitalism, Socialism and Democracy*, New York 1975 (1942), pp. 137, 128. In a similar vein, Weber evoked Carlyle's definition of the age of Cromwell as 'the last of our heroisms' (Weber, *Protestant Ethic*, p. 37).

32   On the relationship between adventure-mentality and the capitalist spirit, see Michael Nerlich, *The Ideology of Adventure: Studies in Modern Consciousness, 1100–1750*, Minnesota 1987 (1977), and the first two sections of the next chapter.

'Not vulgar, or common, though', put in her father . . .[33]

Hardly, about, neither exactly, nor yet, nothing, not quite . . . Margaret's judgment, usually quite sharp, loses itself in a spiral of evasions. It's the *abstraction* of the bourgeois type: in his extreme form, mere 'capital personified', or even just 'a machine for the transformation of surplus-value into surplus capital', to quote a couple of passages from *Capital*.[34] In Marx, as later in Weber, the methodical suppression of all sensuous traits makes it hard to imagine how this character could ever be the centre of an interesting story—unless of course self-repression *is* the story, as in Mann's portrait of consul Thomas Buddenbrook (which made a profound impression on Weber himself).[35] Things are different in an earlier period, or at the margins of capitalist Europe, where the weakness of capitalism as a system leaves much greater freedom to imagine powerful individual figures like Robinson Crusoe, Gesualdo Motta, or Stanislaw Wokulski. But where capitalistic structures solidify, narrative and stylistic mechanisms replace individuals as the centre of the text. It's another way to look at the structure of this book: two chapters on bourgeois characters—and two on bourgeois language.

6. PROSE AND KEYWORDS: PRELIMINARY REMARKS

I found the bourgeois in styles more than stories, I said a few pages ago, and by 'styles' I meant mostly two things: prose, and keywords. The rhetoric of prose will come into view gradually, one aspect at a

---

33 Elizabeth Gaskell, *North and South*, New York/London 2005 (1855), p. 60.

34 Karl Marx, *Capital*, vol. I, Harmondsworth 1990 (1867), pp. 739, 742.

35 On Mann and the bourgeoisie, besides Lukács's numerous essays, see Alberto Asor Rosa's 'Thomas Mann o dell'ambiguità borghese', *Contropiano* 2: 68 and 3: 68. If there is one specific moment when the idea of a book on the bourgeois first crossed my mind, it was over forty years ago, reading Asor's essays; the book was then begun in earnest in 1999–2000, during a year at the Wissenschaftskolleg in Berlin.

time (continuity, precision, productivity, neutrality . . .), in the first
two chapters of the book, where I chart its ascending arc through
the eighteenth and nineteenth centuries. It has been a great achievement, bourgeois prose—and a very *laborious* one. The absence
from its universe of any concept of 'inspiration'—this gift from the
gods, where idea and results merge magically in a single instant of
creation—suggests how impossible it is to imagine the medium of
prose without immediately thinking of *work*. Linguistic work, to be
sure, but of such a kind that it embodies some of the most typical
features of bourgeois activity. If *The Bourgeois* has a protagonist,
this laborious prose is certainly it.

The prose I have just outlined is an ideal-type, never fully realized
in any specific text. Keywords, no; they are actual words, used by
real writers, and perfectly traceable to this or that book. Here, the
conceptual frame has been set decades ago by Raymond Williams,
in *Culture & Society* and *Keywords*, and by Reinhart Koselleck's
work on *Begriffgeschichte*. For Koselleck, who focuses on the political language of modern Europe, 'a concept is not simply indicative
of the relations which it covers; it is also a *factor* within them';[36]
more precisely, it is a factor that institutes a 'tension' between
language and reality, and is often 'consciously deployed as a
weapon'.[37] Though a great model for intellectual history, this
approach is probably unsuited to a social being who, as Groethuysen
puts it, 'acts, but doesn't speak much';[38] and when he speaks, prefers
casual and everyday terms to the intellectual clarity of concepts.
'Weapon' is thus certainly the wrong term for pragmatic and
constructive keywords such as 'useful', 'efficiency', 'serious'—not
to mention great mediators like 'comfort' or 'influence', much
closer to Benveniste's idea of language as 'the instrument by which

---

36   Koselleck, '*Begriffgeschichte* and Social History', p. 86.
37   Ibid., p. 78.
38   Groethuysen, *Origines I*, p. xi.

the world and society are *adjusted*[39] than to Koselleck's 'tension'. It is hardly an accident, I think, that so many of my keywords have turned out to be adjectives: less central than nouns (let alone concepts) to a culture's semantic system, adjectives are unsystematic and indeed 'adjustable'; or, as Humpty Dumpty would scornfully say, 'adjectives, you can do anything with'.[40]

Prose, and keywords: two parallel threads that will resurface throughout the argument, at the different scales of paragraphs, sentences, and individual words. Through them, the peculiarities of bourgeois culture will emerge from the implicit, and even buried dimension of language: a 'mentality' made of unconscious grammatical patterns and semantic associations, more than clear and distinct ideas. This was not the original plan of the book, and there are moments when I'm still taken aback by the fact that the pages on Victorian adjectives may be the conceptual centre of *The Bourgeois*. But if the ideas of the bourgeois have received plenty of attention, his mentality—aside from a few isolated attempts, like Groethuysen's study almost a century ago—remains still largely unexplored; and then, the *minutiae* of language reveal secrets that great ideas often mask: the friction between new aspirations and old habits, the false starts, the hesitations, the compromises; in one word, the *slowness* of cultural history. For a book that sees bourgeois culture as an incomplete project, it felt like the right methodological choice.

7. 'THE BOURGEOIS IS LOST . . .'

On 14 April 1912, Benjamin Guggenheim, Solomon's younger brother, found himself on board the *Titanic*, and, as the ship started

---

39   Emile Benveniste, 'Remarks on the Function of Language in Freudian Theory', in *Problems in General Linguistics*, Oxford, OH, 1971 (1966), p. 71 (emphasis added).

40   Lewis Carroll, *Through the Looking-Glass, and What Alice Found There*, Harmondsworth 1998 (1872), p. 186.

sinking, he was one of those who helped women and children onto the lifeboats, withstanding the frenzy, and at times the brutality, of other male passengers. Then, when his steward was ordered to man one of the boats, Guggenheim took his leave, and asked him to tell his wife that 'no woman was left on board because Ben Guggenheim was a coward'. And that was it.[41] His words may have been a little less resonant, but it really doesn't matter; he did the right, very difficult thing to do. And so, when a researcher for Cameron's 1997 *Titanic* unearthed the anecdote, he immediately brought it to the scriptwriters' attention: what a scene. But he was flatly turned down: too unrealistic. The rich don't die for abstract principles like cowardice and the like. And indeed, the film's vaguely Guggenheim-like figure tries to force his way onto a lifeboat with a gun.

'The bourgeois is lost', wrote Thomas Mann in his 1932 essay on 'Goethe as a Representative of the Bourgeois Age', and these two *Titanic* moments—placed at the opposite ends of the twentieth century—agree with him. Lost, not because capitalism is: to the contrary, capitalism is stronger than ever (if, Golem-like, mostly in destruction). What has evaporated is the sense of bourgeois *legitimacy*: the idea of a ruling class that doesn't just rule, but *deserves* to do so. It was this conviction that animated Guggenheim's words on the *Titanic*; at stake, was his class's 'prestige (and hence trust)', to use one of Gramsci's passages on the concept of hegemony.[42] Giving it up, meant losing the right to rule.

Power, justified by values. But just as bourgeois political rule was finally on the agenda,[43] three major novelties, emerging in

41   John H. Davis, *The Guggenheims, 1848–1988: An American Epic*, New York 1988, p. 221.

42   Antonio Gramsci, *Quaderni del carcere*, Torino 1975, p. 1519.

43   Having been 'the first class in history to achieve economic pre-eminence without aspiring to political rule', writes Hannah Arendt, the bourgeoisie achieved its 'political emancipation' in the course of 'the imperialist period (1886–1914)'.

quick succession, altered the picture forever. First came political collapse. As the *belle époque* came to its tawdry end, like the *operette* in which it liked to mirror itself, the bourgeoisie joined forces with the old elite in precipitating Europe into the carnage of war; afterwards, it shielded its class interests behind black and brown shirts, paving the way for worse massacres. As the old regime was ending, the new men proved incapable of acting like a true ruling class: when, in 1942, Schumpeter wrote with cold contempt that 'the bourgeois class . . . needs a master',[44] he had no need to explain what he meant.

The second transformation, nearly opposite in nature, emerged after the Second World War, with the widespread establishment of democratic regimes. 'The peculiarity of the historical consent won from the masses within modern capitalist social formations', writes Perry Anderson, is

> the belief by the masses that *they exercise an ultimate self-determination* within the existing social order . . . a credence in the democratic equality of all citizens in the government of the nation—in other words, disbelief in the existence of any ruling class.[45]

Having concealed itself behind rows of uniforms, the European bourgeoisie now absconded behind a political myth that demanded its self-effacement as a class; an act of camouflage made that much easier by the pervasive discourse of the 'middle class'. And then, the final touch; as capitalism brought a relative well-being to the lives of large working masses in the West, commodities became the new principle of legitimation: consensus was built on things, not

Hannah Arendt, *The Origins of Totalitarianism*, New York 1994 (1948), p. 123.
44 Schumpeter, *Capitalism, Socialism and Democracy*, p. 138.
45 'The Antinomies of Antonio Gramsci', *New Left Review* I/100 (November–December 1976), p. 30.

men—let alone principles. It was the dawn of today: capitalism triumphant, and bourgeois culture dead.

Many things are missing from this book. Some I had discussed elsewhere, and felt I had nothing new to say about: it's the case of Balzac's *parvenus*, or Dickens's middle class, that had played a large role in *The Way of the World* and *Atlas of the European Novel*. Late-nineteenth-century American authors—Norris, Howells, Dreiser—seemed for their part to add little to the general picture; besides, *The Bourgeois* is a partisan essay, with no encyclopaedic ambitions. That said, there is one topic that I would have really liked to include, had it not threatened to become a book all by itself: a parallel between Victorian Britain and the post-1945 United States, highlighting the paradox of these two hegemonic capitalist cultures—the only ones that have existed so far—resting largely on anti-bourgeois values.[46] I am thinking, of course, of the omnipresence of religious sentiment in public discourse; a presence that is in fact growing, in a sharp reversal of earlier trends towards secularization. Similarly for the great technological advances of the nineteenth and late twentieth century: instead of encouraging a rationalistic mentality, the industrial and then the digital 'revolutions' have produced a mix of scientific illiteracy and religious

---

46   In common use, the term 'hegemony' covers two domains that are historically and logically distinct: the hegemony of one capitalist state over other capitalist states, and that of one social class over other social classes; or in short, international and national hegemony. Britain and the United States have been the only cases of *international* hegemony so far; but of course there have been many cases of national bourgeois classes variously exercising their hegemony at home. My argument in this paragraph and in 'Fog' has to do with the specific values I associate to British and American *national* hegemony; how these values relate to those that foster international hegemony is a very interesting question, just not the one addressed here.

superstition—these, too, worse now than then—that defy belief. In this, the United States of today radicalizes the central thesis of the Victorian chapter: the defeat of Weberian *Entzauberung* at the core of the capitalist system, and its replacement by a sentimental re-enchantment of social relations. In both cases, a key ingredient has been the drastic infantilization of the national culture: from the pious idea of 'family reading' that launched the Bowdlerization of Victorian literature, to the syrupy replica—the family, smiling at its TV—that has put American entertainment to sleep.[47] And the parallel can be extended in just about every direction, from the anti-intellectualism of 'useful' knowledge, and of much educational policy—beginning with its addiction to sports—to the ubiquity of words like 'earnest' (then) and 'fun' (now), with their thinly disguised contempt for intellectual and emotional seriousness.

The 'American way of life' as the Victorianism of today: tempting as the idea was, I was too aware of my ignorance of contemporary matters, and decided against it. It was the right decision—but difficult, because it meant admitting that *The Bourgeois* was an exclusively historical study, with no true link to the present. History professors, muses Dr Cornelius in 'Disorder and Early Sorrow', 'do not love history because it is something that comes to pass, but only because it is something that *has* come to pass . . . their hearts belong to the coherent, disciplined, historic past . . . The past is immortalized; that is to say, it is dead.'[48] Like Cornelius, I too am a history professor; but I like to think that disciplined lifelessness may not be all I will be capable of. In this sense, inscribing *The Bourgeois* to Perry Anderson and Paolo Flores d'Arcais signals more than my friendship and admiration towards them; it expresses the hope that,

---

47   Tellingly, the most representative story-tellers of the two cultures—Dickens and Spielberg—have both specialized in stories that appeal to children as much as to adults.

48   Thomas Mann, *Stories of Three Decades*, New York 1936, p. 506.

one day, I will learn from them to use the intelligence of the past for the critique of the present. This book does not live up to that hope. But the next one may.

I

A Working Master

I. ADVENTURE, ENTERPRISE, *FORTUNA*

The beginning is known: a father warns his son against abandoning the 'middle state'—equally free from 'the labour and suffering of the mechanick part of mankind', and 'the pride, luxury, ambition and envy of the upper part'—to become one of those who go 'abroad upon adventures, to rise by enterprise'.[1] Adventures, and enterprise: together. Because adventure, in *Robinson Crusoe* (1719), means more than the 'strange surprising' occurrences—Shipwreck . . . Pyrates . . . un-inhabited Island . . . the Great River of Oroonoque . . .—of the book's title-page; when Robinson, in his second voyage, carries on board 'a small adventure'[2] the term indicates, not a type of event, but a form of capital. In early modern German, writes Michael Nerlich, 'adventure' belonged to the 'common terminology of trade', where it indicated 'the sense of risk (which was also called *angst*)'.[3] And then, quoting a study by Bruno Kuske: 'A distinction was made between *aventiure* trade and the sale to known customers. *Aventiure* trade covered those cases in

---

1   Daniel Defoe, *Robinson Crusoe*, Harmondsworth 1965 (1719), p. 28.
2   Ibid., p. 39.
3   Nerlich, *The Ideology of Adventure*, p. 57.

which the merchant set off with his goods without knowing
exactly which market he would find for them.'

Adventure as a risky investment: Defoe's novel is a monument to the
idea, and to its association with 'the dynamic tendency of capitalism . . . never really to maintain the *status quo*'.[4] But it's a capitalism
of a particular kind, that which appeals to the young Robinson
Crusoe: as in the case of Weber's 'capitalist adventurer', what captures
his imagination are activities 'of an irrational and speculative character, or directed to acquisition by force'.[5] Acquisition by force is
clearly the story of the island (and of the slave plantation before it);
and as for irrationality, Robinson's frequent acknowledgments of his
'wild and indigested notion' and 'foolish inclination of wandring'[6] is
fully in line with Weber's typology. In this perspective, the first part
of *Robinson Crusoe* is a perfect illustration of the adventure-mentality
of early modern long-distance trade, with its 'risks that [were] not just
high, but incalculable, and, as such, beyond the horizon of rational
capitalist enterprise.'[7]

Beyond the horizon . . . In his legendary lecture at the Biblioteca
Hertziana, in Rome, in 1929, Aby Warburg devoted an entire
panel to the moody goddess of sea trade—*Fortuna*—claiming that
early Renaissance humanism had finally overcome the old mistrust
of her fickleness. Though he recalled the overlap between Fortuna
as 'chance', 'wealth', and 'storm wind' (the Italian *fortunale*),
Warburg presented a series of images in which Fortuna was
progressively losing its demonic traits; most memorably, in
Giovanni Rucellai's coat of arms she was 'standing in a ship and

4   Ian Watt, *The Rise of the Novel: Studies in Defoe, Richardson and Fielding*,
Berkeley, CA, 1957, p. 65.
5   Weber, *Protestant Ethic*, p. 20.
6   Defoe, *Robinson Crusoe*, p. 38.
7   Giovanni Arrighi, *The Long Twentieth Century: Money, Power, and the
Origins of Our Times*, London 1994, p. 122.

acting as its mast, gripping the yard in her left hand and the lower end of a swelling sail in her right.'[8] This image, Warburg went on, had been the answer given by Rucellai himself 'to his own momentous question: Have human reason and practical intelligence any power against the accidents of fate, against Fortune?' In that age 'of growing mastery of the seas', the reply had been in the affirmative: Fortune had become 'calculable and subject to laws', and, as a result, the old 'merchant venturer' had himself turned into the more rational figure of the 'merchant explorer'.[9] It's the same thesis independently advanced by Margaret Cohen in *The Novel and the Sea*: if we think of Robinson as 'a crafty navigator', she writes, his story ceases to be a cautionary tale against 'high-risk activities', and becomes instead a reflection on 'how to undertake them with the best chance of success'.[10] No longer irrationally 'pre'-modern, the young Robinson Crusoe is the genuine beginning of the world of today.

Fortune, rationalized. It's an elegant idea—whose application to *Robinson*, however, misses too large a part of the story to be fully convincing. Storms and pirates, cannibals and captivity, life-threatening shipwrecks and narrow escapes are all episodes

---

8   Aby Warburg, 'Francesco Sassetti's Last Injunctions to his Sons' (1907), in *The Renewal of Pagan Antiquity*, Los Angeles 1999, pp. 458, 241. In the arrangement devised for the lecture, and reproduced in 1998 in Siena at the exhibition 'Mnemosyne', this was panel 48.

9   Warburg alludes here to the Merchant Adventurers, the most successful commercial group of early modern England. Despite their name, the Adventurers weren't adventurous at all: protected by a royal charter, they monopolized the export of English woollen cloth to the Low Countries and the German territories (though they had lost most of their power by the outbreak of the Civil War). In a total change of routes and staples, Robinson makes his fortune with the sugar trade of the slave economies of the Atlantic. On early modern merchant groups, see Robert Brenner's splendid *Merchants and Revolution: Commercial Change, Political Conflict, and London's Overseas Traders, 1550–1653*, London 2003 (1993).

10   Margaret Cohen, *The Novel and the Sea*, Princeton 2010, p. 63.

in which it's impossible to discern the sign of Cohen's 'craft', or Warburg's 'mastery of the sea'; while the early scene where ships are 'driven . . . at all adventures, and that with not a mast standing'[11] reads like the striking reversal of Rucellai's coat of arms. As for Robinson's financial success, its modernity is at least as questionable: though the magic paraphernalia of the story of Fortunatus (who had been his main predecessor in the pantheon of modern self-made men) are gone from the novel, the way in which Robinson's wealth piles up in his absence and is later returned—'an old pouch' filled with 'one hundred and sixty Portugal moidores in gold', followed by 'seven fine leopards' skins . . . five chests of excellent sweetmeats, a hundred pieces of gold uncoined . . . one thousand two hundred chests of sugar, eight hundred rolls of tobacco, and the rest of the whole account in gold'—is still very much the stuff of fairy tales.[12]

Let me be clear, Defoe's novel *is* a great modern myth; but it is so *despite* its adventures, and not because of them. When William Empson, in *Some Versions of Pastoral*, offhandedly compared Robinson to Sinbad the Sailor, he had it exactly right;[13] if anything, Sinbad's desire 'to trade . . . and to earn my living'[14] is more explicitly—and rationally—mercantile than Robinson's 'meer wandring inclination'. Where the similarity between the two stories ends is not on the sea; it's on land. In each of his seven voyages, the Baghdad merchant is trapped on as many enchanted islands—ogres, carnivorous beasts, malevolent apes, murderous magicians . . .—from which he can only escape with a further leap into the unknown (as when he ties himself to the claw of a giant carnivorous bird). In

---

11   Defoe, *Robinson Crusoe*, p. 34.

12   Ibid., p. 280.

13   William Empson, *Some Versions of Pastoral*, New York 1974 (1935), p. 204.

14   *The Arabian Nights: Tales of 1001 Nights*, Harmondsworth 2010, vol. II, p. 464.

Sinbad, in other words, adventures rule the sea, and the terra firma as well. In *Robinson*, no. On land, it is work that rules.

2. 'This will testify for me that I was not idle'

But why work? At first, to be sure, it's a matter of survival: a situation in which 'the day's tasks . . . seem to disclose themselves, by the logic of need, before the labourer's eyes'.[15] But even when his future needs are secure 'as long as I lived . . . if it were to be forty years',[16] Robinson just keeps toiling, steadily, page after page. His real-life model Alexander Selkirk had (supposedly) spent his four years on Juan Fernandez oscillating madly between being 'dejected, languid, and melancholy', and plunging into 'one continual Feast . . . equal to the most sensual Pleasures'.[17] Robinson, not even once. In the course of the eighteenth century, it has been calculated, the number of yearly workdays rose from 250 to 300; on his island, where the status of Sunday is never completely clear, the total is certainly higher.[18] When, at the height of his zeal—'You are to understand that now I had . . . two plantations . . . several apartments or caves . . . two pieces of corn-ground . . . my country seat . . . my enclosure for my cattle . . . a living magazine of

---

15   Stuart Sherman, *Telling Time: Clocks, Diaries, and English Diurnal Forms, 1660–1785*, Chicago 1996, p. 228. Sherman is quoting, with a slight modification, E. P. Thompson's words in 'Time, Work-Discipline, and Industrial Capitalism', *Past & Present* 38 (December 1967), p. 59.

16   Defoe, *Robinson Crusoe*, p. 161.

17   I am quoting Steele's description of Selkirk in *The Englishman* 26 (3 December 1713); now in Rae Blanchard, ed., *The Englishman: A Political Journal by Richard Steele*, Oxford 1955, pp. 107–8.

18   Joyce Appleby, *The Relentless Revolution: A History of Capitalism*, New York 2010, p. 106. According to other reconstructions (for instance, Jan de Vries, *The Industrious Revolution: Consumer Behavior and the Household Economy, 1650 to the Present*, Cambridge 2008, pp. 87–8), what increased in the eighteenth century was not the number of workdays, which had already reached the threshold of 300 or so, but that of daily work hours; as we will see, however, Robinson seems to be well ahead of his times even in this respect.

flesh . . . my winter store of raisins'[19]—he turns to the reader and exclaims, 'this will testify for me that I was not idle', one can only nod in agreement. And, then, repeat the question: Why *does* he work so much?

'We scarcely realize today what a unique and astonishing phenomenon a "working" upper class is', writes Norbert Elias in *The Civilizing Process*: 'why submit itself to this compulsion even though it is . . . not commanded by a superior to do so?'[20] Elias's wonder is shared by Alexandre Kojève, who discerns at the centre of Hegel's *Phenomenology* a paradox—'the Bourgeois's problem'—whereby the bourgeois must simultaneously 'work for *another*' (because work only arises as a result of an external constraint), yet can only 'work for *himself*' (because he no longer has a master).[21] Working for himself, *as if he were another*: this is exactly how Robinson functions: one side of him becomes a carpenter, or potter, or baker, and spends weeks and weeks trying to accomplish something; then Crusoe the master emerges, and points out the inadequacy of the results. And then the cycle repeats itself all over again. And it repeats itself, because work has become *the new principle of legitimation of social power*. When, at the end of the novel, Robinson finds himself 'master . . . of above five thousand pounds sterling'[22] and of all the rest, his twenty-eight years of uninterrupted toil are there *to justify his fortune*. Realistically, there is no relationship between the two: he is rich because of the exploitation of nameless slaves in his Brazilian plantation—whereas his solitary labour hasn't brought him a single pound. But we have seen him work like no other character in fiction: How can he not *deserve* what he has?[23]

19   Defoe, *Robinson Crusoe*, pp. 160–1.
20   Norbert Elias, *The Civilizing Process*, Oxford 2000 (1939), p. 128.
21   Alexandre Kojève, *Introduction to the Reading of Hegel: Lectures on the 'Phenomenology of Spirit'*, Ithaca, NY, 1969 (1947), p. 65.
22   Defoe, *Robinson Crusoe*, p. 280.
23   'What he has' includes of course the island, too: 'His *labour* hath taken it

There is a word that perfectly captures Robinson's behaviour: 'industry'. According to the OED, its initial meaning, around 1500, was that of 'intelligent or clever working; skill, ingenuity, dexterity, or cleverness'. Then, in the mid-sixteenth century, a second meaning emerges—'diligence or assiduity . . . close and steady application . . . exertion, effort', that soon crystallizes as 'systematic work or labour; habitual employment in some useful work'.[24] From skill and ingenuity, to systematic exertion; this is how 'industry' contributes to bourgeois culture: hard work, replacing the clever variety.[25] And *calm* work, too, in the same sense that interest is for Hirschmann a 'calm passion': steady, methodical, cumulative, and thus stronger

---

out of the hands of nature', writes Locke about uncultivated land in the chapter 'Of Property' of the *Second Treatise*, 'where it was common, and belong'd equally to all her children, and *hath* thereby *appropriated* it to himself.' By working on the island, in other words, Robinson has made it his own. John Locke, *Two Treatises on Government*, Cambridge 1960 (1690), p. 331.

24 My thanks to Sue Laizik, who first made me aware of these metamorphoses. 'Industry' is of course one of Raymond Williams's keywords in *Culture and Society*; the transformation that most interests him, though—the fact that industry becomes 'a thing in itself—an institution, a body of activities— rather than simply a human attribute'—occurs after the one described here, and probably as its consequence: first industry becomes the simple abstract labour that anyone can perform (in contrast to the uniqueness of 'skill and ingenuity'); then it is abstracted a second time, becoming a 'thing in itself'. See Raymond Williams, *Culture & Society: 1780–1950*, New York 1983 (1958), p. xiii, and the entry 'Industry' in his *Keywords: A Vocabulary of Culture and Society*, rev. edn, Oxford 1983 (1976).

25 As the adjective 'industrious' makes clear, hard work possesses in English an ethical halo that 'clever' work lacks; which explains why the legendary firm of Arthur Andersen Accounting still included 'hard work' in its 'table of values' in the 1990s—while the clever arm of the same firm (Anderson Counseling, which had been concocting all sorts of investment practices) replaced it with 'respect for individuals', which is neoliberal Newspeak for financial bonuses. Eventually, Counseling strong-armed Accounting into validating stock value manipulation, thus leading to the firm's shameful downfall. See Susan E. Squires, Cynthia J. Smith, Lorma McDougall and William R. Yeack, *Inside Arthur Andersen: Shifting Values, Unexpected Consequences*, New York 2003, pp. 90–1.

than the 'turbulent (yet weak) passions' of the old aristocracy.[26] Here, the discontinuity between the two ruling classes is unmistakable: if turbulent passions had idealized what was needed by a warlike caste—the white heat of the brief 'day' of battle—bourgeois interest is the virtue of a peaceful and repeatable (and repeatable, and repeatable, and repeatable) everyday: less energy, but for a much longer time. A few hours—'about four in the evening', writes Robinson, ever modest[27]—but for twenty-eight years.

In the previous section, we have looked at the adventures that open *Robinson Crusoe*; in this one, at the work of his life on the island. It's the same progression of *The Protestant Ethic*: a history that begins with the 'capitalist adventurer', but where the ethos of laboriousness eventually brings about the 'rational tempering of his irrational impulse'.[28] In the case of Defoe, the transition from the first to the second figure is particularly striking, because apparently wholly unplanned: on the title-page of the novel (Figure 2), Robinson's 'strange surprising adventures'—mentioned at the top, and in larger size—are clearly billed as the main attraction, whereas the part on the island is simply 'one of the many other episodes'.[29] But then, during the composition of the novel, an 'unforeseen, uncontrolled expansion' of the island must have occurred, which shook off its subordination to the story of adventures and made it the new centre of the text. A Calvinist from Geneva was the first to grasp the significance of this mid-course re-orientation: Rousseau's *Robinson*,

---

26   Albert O. Hirschmann, *The Passions and the Interests: Political Arguments for Capitalism before its Triumph*, Princeton, NJ 1997 (1977), pp. 65–6.

27   Defoe, *Robinson Crusoe*, p. 127. The three hours of hunting 'in the morning', and the 'ordering, curing, preserving and cooking' that take a 'great part of the day' should clearly be added to the four in the evening, producing a tally well above that of most labourers of his time.

28   Ibid., p. 17.

29   It's a point I owe to Giuseppe Sertoli, 'I due Robinson', in *Le avventure di Robinson Crusoe*, Turin 1998, p. xiv.

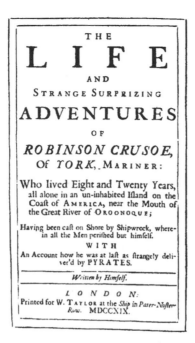

THE

L I F E

AND

STRANGE SURPRIZING

ADVENTURES

OF

ROBINSON CRUSOE,

Of *TORK,* MARINER:

Who lived Eight and Twenty Years,
all alone in an un-inhabited Ifland on the
Coaft of AMERICA, near the Mouth of
the Great River of OROONOQUE;

Having been caft on Shore by Shipwreck, wherein all the Men perifhed but himfelf.

WITH

An Account how he was at laft as ftrangely deli-
ver'd by PYRATES.

Written by Himfelf.

L O N D O N:
Printed for W. TAYLOR at the *Ship* in *Pater-Nofter-
Row.* MDCCXIX.

Figure 2

'cleansed of all its claptrap', will begin with the shipwreck, and be
limited to the years on the island, so that Emile will not waste his
time in dreams of adventure, and may concentrate instead on
Robinson's work ('he will want to know all that is useful, and nothing but that').[30] Which is cruel to Emile, of course, and to all children
after him, but right: because Robinson's hard work on the island is
indeed the greatest novelty of the book.

From the capitalist adventurer, to the working master. But then, as
Robinson approaches the end, a second about-face occurs: cannibals,
armed conflict, mutineers, wolves, bears, fairy-tale fortune . . .
Why? If the poetics of adventure had been 'tempered' by its rational

---

30   Jean-Jacques Rousseau, *Emile* (1762), in *Oeuvres complètes*, Paris 1969,
vol. IV, pp. 455–6.

opposite, why promise 'some very surprising incidents in some new adventures of my own' *in the very last sentence of the novel*?[31]

So far, I have emphasized the opposition between the culture of adventures and the rational work ethic; and I have indeed no doubt that the two are incompatible, and that the latter is the more recent phenomenon, specific to modern European capitalism. That however does not mean that modern capitalism can be *reduced* to the work ethic, as Weber was clearly inclined to do; by the same token, the fact that activities 'of an irrational and speculative character, or directed to acquisition by force' are no longer *typical* of modern capitalism does not mean that they are *absent* from it. A variety of non-economic practices, violent and often unpredictable in their results—Marx's 'primitive accumulation', or David Harvey's recent 'accumulation by dispossession'—have clearly played (and in fact *still* play) a major role in the expansion of capitalism; and if this is so, then a narrative of adventure, broadly construed—like for instance, in a later age, Conrad's *entrelacement* of metropolitan reflection and colonial romance—is still perfectly appropriate to the representation of modernity.

This, then, is the historical basis for the 'two Robinsons', and the ensuing discontinuity in the structure of Defoe's narrative: the island offers the first glimpse of the industrious master of modern times; the sea, Africa, Brazil, Friday, and the other adventures give voice to the older—but never fully discarded—forms of capitalist domination. From a formal viewpoint, this coexistence-without-integration of opposite registers—so unlike Conrad's calculated

---

31 'The *Farther Adventures of Robinson Crusoe*', writes Maximilian Novak, 'was published on 20 August 1719, approximately four months after the appearance of the first volume'; a fact that strongly suggests that Defoe 'was already at work on the sequel before the original was printed', and that therefore that last sentence is not an idle flourish, but a very concrete advertising move. See Maximillian E. Novak, *Daniel Defoe: Master of Fictions*, Oxford 2001, p. 555.

hierarchy, to use that parallel again—is clearly a flaw of the novel. But, just as clearly, the inconsistency *is not just a matter of form*: it arises from the unresolved dialectic of the bourgeois type himself, and of his two 'souls':[32] suggesting, contra Weber, that the rational bourgeois will never truly outgrow his irrational impulses, nor repudiate the predator he once used to be. In being, not just the beginning of a new era, but a beginning *in which a structural contradiction becomes visible that will be never overcome*, Defoe's shapeless story remains the great classic of bourgeois literature.

3. KEYWORDS I: 'USEFUL'

Nov. 4. This morning I began to order my times of work, of going out with my gun, time of sleep, and time of diversion, viz. every morning I walked out with my gun for two or three hours if it did not rain, then employed my self to work till about eleven a-clock, then eat what I had to live on, and from twelve to two I lay down to sleep, the weather being excessive hot, and then in the evening to work again.[33]

Work, gun, sleep, and diversion. But when Robinson actually describes his day, diversion disappears, and his life recalls to the letter Hegel's crisp summary of the Enlightenment: here, 'everything is *useful*'.[34] Useful: the first keyword of this book. When Robinson returns on board the ship after the shipwreck, its

---

32   The metaphor of the 'two souls'—inspired by a famous monologue of *Faust*—is the leitmotif of Sombart's book on the bourgeois: 'Two souls dwell in the breast of every complete bourgeois: the soul of the entrepreneur and the soul of the respectable middle-class man . . . the spirit of enterprise is a synthesis of the greed of gold, the desire for adventure, the love of exploration . . . the bourgeois spirit is composed of calculation, careful policy, reasonableness, and economy'. Werner Sombart, *The Quintessence of Capitalism*, London 1915 (1913), pp. 202, 22.

33   Defoe, *Robinson Crusoe*, pp. 88–9.

34   G. W. F. Hegel, *Phenomenology of Spirit*, Oxford 1979 (1807), p. 342.

incantatory repetition—from the carpenter's chest, 'which was a very useful prize to me', to the 'several things very useful to me', and 'everything . . . that could be useful to me'[35]—re-orients the world by placing Robinson at its center (useful *to me . . . to me . . . to me . . .*). The useful is here, as in Locke, the category that at once establishes private property (useful *to me*), and legitimates it by identifying it with work (*useful* to me). Tullio Pericoli's illustrations for the novel, which look like deranged versions of the technological *tableaux* of the *Encyclopèdie* (Figure 3),[36] capture the essence of this world in which no object is an end in itself—in the kingdom of the useful, *nothing* is an end in itself—but always and only *a means to do something else.* A tool. And in a world of tools, there is only one thing left to do: work.[37]

Everything for him. Everything a tool. And then, the third dimension of the useful:

> At last, being eager to view the circumference of my little kingdom, I resolved upon my cruise; and accordingly I victualled my ship for the voyage, putting in two dozen of loaves (cakes I should call them) of barley-bread, an earthen pot full of parched rice (a food I ate a good deal of), a little bottle of rum, half a goat, and powder and shot for killing more, and two large watch-coats, of those which, as I mentioned before, I had saved out of the seamen's chests; these I took, one to lie upon, and the other to cover me in the night.[38]

---

35   Defoe, *Robinson Crusoe*, pp. 69ff.

36   Tullio Pericoli, *Robinson Crusoe di Daniel Defoe*, Milan 2007.

37   In such a world of tools, human beings become themselves tools—that is to say, mere cogs in the social division of labour; thus, Robinson never evokes the other sailors by name, but only by activity: seaman, carpenter, gunner . . .

38   Defoe, *Robinson Crusoe*, p. 147.

Figure 3

Here, next to Robinson as the active centre of the story (*I* resolved . . . *I* victualled . . . *I* had saved . . . *I* took . . .), and to the objects he needs for the expedition (an earthen pot . . . powder and shot . . . two large watch-coats . . .), a cascade of final constructions—for the voyage . . . for killing more . . . to lie upon . . . to cover me—completes the triangle of the useful. Subject, object, *and verb*. A verb that has interiorized the lesson of tools, and reproduces it within Robinson's activity itself: where an action, typically, is always done *in order to do something else*:

Accordingly, the next day I went to my country house, as I called it, and cutting some of the smaller twigs, I found them to my purpose as much as I could desire; whereupon I came the next time prepared with a hatchet to cut down a quantity, which I soon found, for there was great plenty of them. These I set up to dry within my circle or hedge, and when they were fit for use I carried them to my cave; and here, during the next season, I employed myself in making, as well as I could, a great many baskets, both to carry earth or to carry or lay up anything, as I had occasion; and though I did not finish them very handsomely, yet I made them sufficiently serviceable for my purpose; thus, afterwards, I took care never to be without them; and as my wicker-ware decayed, I made more, especially strong, deep baskets to place my corn in, instead of sacks, when I should come to have any quantity of it.

Having mastered this difficulty, and employed a world of time about it, I bestirred myself to see, if possible, how to supply two wants . . .[39]

Two, three verbs per line; in the hands of another writer, so much activity may become frantic. Here, though, a ubiquitous lexicon of teleology (accordingly, purpose, desire, prepared, fit, employed, serviceable, care, supply . . .) provides a connective tissue that makes the page consistent and solid, while verbs pragmatically subdivide Robinson's actions into the immediate tasks of the main clauses (I went, I found, I came, I set up), and the more indefinite future of its final clauses (to cut down . . . to carry . . . to place . . . to supply . . .); though not *much* more indefinite, to be sure, because the ideal future, for a culture of the useful, is one so close at hand, as to be little more than the continuation of the present: 'the *next* day'; 'the *next* season'; 'to cut down a quantity, *which I soon found*'. All is tight and concatenated, here; no step is ever skipped ('whereupon— I came—the next time—prepared—with a hatchet—to cut down—a quantity') in these sentences that, like Hegel's 'prosaic mind', understand the world via 'categories such as cause and effect, or means and end'.[40] *Especially* means and end: *Zweckrationalität*,

39   Ibid., p. 120.
40   G. W. F. Hegel, *Aesthetics: Lectures on Fine Art*, Oxford 1998, vol. II, p.

Weber will call it; rationality directed to, and governed by its aim; 'instrumental reason', in Horkheimer's variation. Two centuries before Weber, Defoe's page illustrates the lexico-grammatical concatenations that were the first embodiment of *Zweckrationalität*: instrumental reason as a *practice of language*—perfectly articulated, though completely unnoticed—well before it became a concept. It's a first glimpse of bourgeois 'mentality', and of Defoe's great contribution to it: prose, as the style of the useful.

4. KEYWORDS II: 'EFFICIENCY'

The style of the useful. A novelist as great as Defoe devoted his last, most ambitious novel entirely to this idea. Emile will want to know all that is useful, Rousseau had written, *and nothing but that*; and Goethe—alas—observed the second clause to the letter. 'From the Useful by Way of the True to the Beautiful', we read at the beginning of the *Wanderjahre* (1829);[41] a novel where, instead of the usual 'pleasure garden or modern park', one finds 'fields of vegetables, large beds of medicinal herbs, and anything that may be useful in any way'.[42] Gone is the conflict between the useful and the beautiful that had been the key to the previous novel about Wilhelm Meister, the *Apprenticeship* of 1796; in the 'Pedagogical Province' of the *Wanderjahre* conflict has given way to functional subordination; having 'chosen to be useful',[43] explains one of the few artists present in the novel, a sculptor, he is now perfectly happy to make anatomical models, and nothing else. The fact that art has been deprived of its recently acquired purposelessness is repeatedly presented as a commendable progress: 'as salt is to food, so are the arts to technical science. We want from art only enough to insure that our handicraft

---

974.
41   Johann Wolfgang Goethe, *Wilhelm Meister's Journeyman Years, or The Renunciants*, New York 1989 (1829), p. 138.
42   Ibid., p. 126.
43   Ibid., p. 326.

will remain in good taste', writes the Abbé to Wilhelm;[44] 'the rigorous arts'—stonecutters, masons, carpenters, roofers, locksmiths . . .
—adds another leader of the Province, 'must set an example for the
free arts, and seek to put them to shame'.[45] And then, if necessary,
the punitive, anti-aesthetic side of Utopia makes its appearance: if
he sees no theatres around, Wilhelm's guide curtly informs him, it's
because 'we found such impostures thoroughly dangerous . . . and
could in no way reconcile them with our serious purpose'.[46] So,
drama is banned from the Province. And that's it.

'The Renunciants', reads the subtitle of the *Wanderjahre*, indicating
with that word the sacrifice of human fullness imposed by the modern
division of labour. Thirty years earlier, in the *Apprenticeship*, the theme
had been presented as a painful mutilation of bourgeois existence;[47] but
in the later novel, pain has disappeared: 'the day for specialization has
come', Wilhelm is immediately told by one of his old associates;
'fortunate is he who comprehends it and labors in this spirit'.[48] The day
has come, and falling in step is a 'fortune'. 'Happy the man whose
vocation becomes his favorite pastime', exclaims a farmer who has
gathered a collection of agricultural tools, 'so that he takes pleasure in
that which his station also makes a duty'.[49] A museum of tools, to celebrate the division of labour. 'All activity, all art . . . can only be
acquired through limitation. To know one thing properly . . . results
in higher cultivation than half-competence in a hundred different

44   Ibid., p. 266.
45   Ibid., p. 383.
46   Ibid., p. 276.
47   Forced to 'develop some of his capabilities, in order to be useful', writes
Wilhelm in his letter to Werner, the bourgeois is condemned to have 'no harmony
in his being: in order to make himself useful in one way, he must disregard
everything else'. Johann Wolfgang Goethe, *Wilhelm Meister's Apprenticeship*,
Princeton, NJ, 1995 (1796), pp. 174–5.
48   Goethe, *Wilhelm Meister's Journeyman Years*, p. 118.
49   Ibid., p. 190.

fields', says one of Wilhelm's interlocutors.[50] 'Where I am useful, there is my fatherland!',[51] adds another and then goes on: 'If I now say, "let each strive to be useful to himself and others in all ways", it is neither a doctrine nor advice, but the maxim of life itself.'

There is a word that would have been perfect for the *Wanderjahre*—had it only existed at the time Goethe was writing: efficiency. Or better, the word did exist, but it still indicated what it had for centuries: 'the fact of being an operative agent or efficient cause', as the OED puts it: efficiency as *causation*, and nothing more. Then, around the mid nineteenth century, the shift: 'fitness or power to accomplish, or success in accomplishing, the purpose intended; adequate power, effectiveness, efficacy.'[52] *Adequate* power: no longer the mere capacity to *do* something, but to do it without any waste, and in the most economic way. If the useful had turned the world into a collection of tools, the division of labour steps in to calibrate the tools towards their ends ('the purpose intended')—and 'efficiency' is the result. They are three consecutive steps in the history of capitalist rationalization.

Of capitalist rationalization—and of European colonialism. 'These chaps were not much account, really', says Marlow, dismissively, of the Romans in Britain; 'they were conquerors, and for that you want only brute force'.[53] Brute force; by contrast, 'what saves' British rule in the colonies is 'efficiency—the devotion to efficiency'.[54] Two mentions, in crescendo, within a single sentence; then the word disappears from *Heart of Darkness*; in its place, a stunningly *in*-efficient

---

50   Ibid., p. 197.
51   Ibid., p. 365.
52   The shift occurs more or less simultaneously in several fields; the OED provides examples from the law (Whately, 1818–60), the history of civilization (Buckle, 1858), political philosophy (Mill, 1859), and political economy (Fawcett, 1863).
53   Joseph Conrad, *Heart of Darkness*, Harmondsworth 1991 (1899), p. 31.
54   Ibid.

world where machines are left to rust and disintegrate, workers gather water with pails that have holes at the bottom, bricks lack the crucial ingredient, and Marlow's own work is halted for lack of rivets (though 'there were cases of them down at the coast—cases—piled up— burst—split!'[55]). And the reason for all this waste is simple: slavery. Slavery was never 'ordered around the idea of efficiency', writes Roberto Schwarz about the Brazilian plantations of Conrad's time, because it could always rely 'on violence and military discipline'; therefore, 'the rational study and continuous modernization of the processes of production' made literally 'no sense'. In such cases, as in the Congo of the 'company', the 'brute force' of the Romans may turn out to be more perversely 'efficient' than efficiency itself.

Strange experiment, *Heart of Darkness*: sending a clear-sighted bourgeois engineer to witness the fact that one of the most profitable ventures of *fin-de-siècle* capitalism was the opposite of industrial efficiency: 'the opposite of what was modern', to quote Schwarz one more time. 'Acquisition by force' survived side by side with modern rationality, I wrote a few pages ago, and Conrad's novella—where the ethical bourgeois is sent to rescue the irrational adventurer—is the perfect example of that jarring cohabitation. Surrounded by a crowd with whom he has nothing in common, Marlow's only moment of empathy is with an anonymous pamphlet he finds in an abandoned station along the river; 'humble pages', he writes, made 'luminous' by their 'honest concern for the right way of going to work'. The *right* way: work ethic, in the midst of colonial pillage. 'Luminous', versus the 'darkness' of the title: religious associations, like those of the 'calling' in *The Protestant Ethic*, or that initial '*devotion* to efficiency', which has its own Weberian echo in the 'devotion to the task' of 'Science as a Profession'. But . . . devotion to efficiency—*in the Congo Free State*? Nothing in common, I said, between Marlow and the plunderers around him: nothing in

---

55   Ibid., p. 58.

common, that is, *except for the fact that he works for them*. The greater his devotion to efficiency, the easier their looting.

The creation of a culture of work has been, arguably, the greatest symbolic achievement of the bourgeoisie as a class: the useful, the division of labour, 'industry', efficiency, the 'calling', the 'seriousness' of the next chapter—all these, and more, bear witness to the enormous significance acquired by what used to be merely a hard necessity or a brutal duty; that Max Weber could use exactly the same concepts to describe manual labour (in *The Protestant Ethic*) and great science (in 'Science as a Profession') is itself a further, indirect sign of the new symbolic value of bourgeois work. But when Marlow's wholehearted devotion to his task turns into the instrument of bloody oppression—a fact so patent, in *Heart of Darkness*, as to be almost invisible—the fundamental antinomy of bourgeois work comes to the surface: the same self-referential absorption that is the source of its greatness—unknown tribes hiding ashore, foolish and frightened murderers on board, and Marlow, oblivious to all, keeping the steamer on course—is the source of its servitude, too. Marlow's work ethic impels him to do his work well; to what end, is not its concern. Like the 'blinders' so memorably evoked in 'Science as a Profession', the legitimacy and productivity of modern work are not just intensified, but *established* by their blindness to what lies around it. It is truly, as Weber writes in *The Protestant Ethic*, an 'irrational sort of life . . . where a man exists for the sake of his business, instead of the reverse', and where the only result of one's ceaseless activity is 'the irrational sense of having done his job well'.[56]

---

56   Weber, *Protestant Ethic*, pp. 70–1. The word 'irrational' haunts Weber's description of the capitalist ethos. But for him there are two opposite kinds of capitalist irrationality: that of the 'adventurer'—where the means are indeed irrational, but the aim (the personal enjoyment of gain) is not—and that of the modern capitalist, where by contrast the means have been thoroughly rationalized, but the result—'a man existing for the sake of his business, instead of the

An irrational sort of life, that dominated by *Zweckrationalität*. But instrumental reason, as we have seen, is also one of the underlying principles of modern prose. In a few pages, the consequences of this association will become visible.

5. KEYWORDS III: 'COMFORT'

Christian asceticism, we read in *The Protestant Ethic*,

> had already ruled the world which it had renounced from the monastery and through the Church. But it had, on the whole, left the naturally spontaneous character of daily life in the world untouched. Now it strode into the market-place of life, slammed the door of the monastery behind it, and undertook to penetrate just that daily routine of life with its methodicalness, to fashion it into a life in the world, but neither of nor for this world.[57]

A life in the world, but neither of nor for the world. Just like Robinson's life: 'in' the island, but neither 'of' nor 'for' the island. And yet, we never have the impression that he 'gets nothing out of [his activity] except the irrational sense of having done his job well', as Weber writes of the capitalist ethos.[58] There is a subdued, elusive sense of enjoyment that pervades the novel—and that is probably one reason for its success. But enjoyment *of what?*

Earlier on, I quoted the moment when Robinson addresses the reader—'this will testify for me that I was not idle'—in the tone of one who is justifying himself in front of a judge. But then, the sentence veers in an unexpected direction: . . . that I was not idle,

---

reverse'—is completely irrational. It's only in the latter case that the absurdity of instrumental reason reveals itself.

57   Ibid., p. 154.
58   Ibid., p. 71.

and that I spared no pains to bring to pass whatever appeared necessary for my comfortable support'.[59] Comfortable: this is the key. If
the 'useful' had transformed the island into a workshop, 'comfort'
restores an element of pleasure to Robinson's existence; under its
sign, even *The Protestant Ethic* finds a lighter moment:

> Worldly Protestant asceticism acted powerfully against the sponta-
> neous enjoyment of possessions; it restricted consumption,
> especially of luxuries . . . On the other hand . . . it did not wish to
> impose mortification on the man of wealth, but the use of his means
> for necessary and practical things. The idea of comfort [*in English in
> the original*] characteristically limits the extent of ethically permis-
> sible expenditures. It is naturally no accident that the development
> of a manner of living consistent with that idea may be observed
> earliest and most clearly among the most consistent representatives
> of this whole attitude towards life. Over against the glitter and
> ostentation of feudal magnificence which, resting on an unsound
> economic basis, prefers a sordid elegance to a sober simplicity, they
> set the clean and solid comfort [*Bequemlichkeit*] of the middle-class
> home [*bürgerlichen 'home'*] as an ideal.[60]

The bourgeois home—the *English* bourgeois home—as the embodiment of comfort. In the course of the eighteenth century, writes
Charles Morazé in *Les bourgeois conquerants*, 'England made fashionable a new type of happiness—that of being at home: the English call
it "comfort", and so will the rest of the world.'[61] Needless to say, there

---

59   Defoe, *Robinson Crusoe*, p. 161.

60   Weber, *Protestant Ethic*, pp. 170–1.

61   Charles Morazé, *Les bourgeois conquerants*, Paris 1957, p. 13. By
Victorian times, the association between home and comfort had become so self-
evident that Peter Gay reports the case of 'an English client' who asked his
architect, in all seriousness, for 'no style at all but the comfortable style' (*Pleasure
Wars*, p. 222). One thinks of Mr Wilcox, in *Howards End*, showing his house to
Margaret Schlegel: 'I can't stand those people who run down comforts . . .

is no 'middle-class home' on Robinson's island; but when he resolves
to make 'such necessary things as I found I most wanted, particularly
a chair and a table; for without these I was not able to enjoy the few
comforts I had in the world',[62] or when he later declares that 'my habitation grew comfortable to me beyond measure',[63] he, too, is clearly
identifying comfort with the domestic horizon: a chair, a table, a pipe,
a notebook . . . an umbrella![64]

Comfort. The origin of the word is in a late Latin compound—
cum + *forte*— that first appears in English in the thirteenth century,
to indicate 'strengthening; encouragement . . . aid, succour'
(OED), and whose semantic sphere remains more or less the same
for another four centuries: 'physical refreshment or sustenance',
'relief', 'aid in want, pain, sickness . . . mental distress or afflic-
tion'. Then, in the late seventeenth century, the sea-change:
comfort is no longer what returns us to a 'normal' state from
adverse circumstances, but what takes normality as its starting
point *and pursues well-being as an end in itself*, independently of
any mishap: 'a thing that produces or ministers to enjoyment and
content (usually, plural, distinguished from necessaries on the one
hand, and from luxuries on the other)'.[65]

---

reasonable comforts, of course.' E. M. Forster, *Howards End*, New York 1998,
pp. 117–18.
   62   Defoe, *Robinson Crusoe*, p. 85.
   63   Ibid., p. 222.
   64   Ibid., p. 145.
   65   As is often the case with semantic change, the old sense and the new
coexist for some time, even in the same text: in Defoe, for instance, the noun and
the verb still convey the old meaning of the term (as when the shipwrecked
Robinson relates how he 'got to the mainland, where, to my great comfort, I
clambered up the cliffs' [p. 65]), while the adjective and adverb incline towards
the new, as when Robinson states that 'my habitation grew comfortable to me
beyond measure' (p. 222), or utters a placid 'thus I lived mighty comfortably',
after having managed to make an umbrella (p. 145).

Necessaries on one side, and luxuries on the other. Caught between such powerful concepts, the idea was bound to become a battlefield. 'The Comforts of Life are so various and extensive', states the wonderful 'Remark (L.)' of *The Fable of the Bees*, 'that no body can tell what People mean by them, except he knows what sort of Life they lead . . . I am apt to believe that when they pray for their daily Bread, the Bishop includes several things in that Petition which the Sexton does not think on'.[66] In the mouth of a bishop, 'comforts' are likely to be luxuries in disguise; this is certainly how the nameless hero of the opening pages of *Pilgrim's Progress*—who receives the name of 'Christian' in the act of forsaking them—understands the term.[67] But grim Benjamin Franklin, for his part, hesitates: '*Friends and Countrymen*', proclaims the *Poor Richard's Almanack* for 1756, 'you spend yearly at least *Two Hundred Thousand Pounds*, 'tis said, in *European, East-Indian* and *West-Indian* Commodities: supposing one Half of this Expence to be in *Things absolutely necessary*, the other Half may be call'd *Superfluities*, or at best, Conveniences, which however you might live without for one little Year.'[68] One little year is the period one can reasonably be asked to abstain from conveniences. Conveniences? 'The words Decency and Conveniency' are so full of 'obscurity', notes Mandeville, implacable, that they are completely useless. And the OED proves him right: 'Convenience: The quality of being . . . suitable or well-adapted to the performance of some action'; 'material arrangements or appliances conducive to personal comfort, ease of action'. If comfort was elusive, this one is worse.[69]

---

66 Bernard Mandeville, *The Fable of the Bees*, London 1980 (1714), pp. 136–7.

67 '"*What!* said *Obstinate*, and leave our Friends, and our comforts behind us!*". "Yes, said *Christian* (for that was his name) because, that all, which you shall forsake, is not worthy to be compared with a little of that that I am seeking to enjoy."' John Bunyan, *The Pilgrim's Progress*, New York/London 2009 (1678), p. 13.

68 Benjamin Franklin, *Autobiography, Poor Richard, and Later Writings*, New York 1987, p. 545.

69 There is in fact a reasonably clear difference between the idea of comfort

Wars of words are always confusing. So, let's re-read that passage from *Robinson Crusoe*: 'I began to apply myself to make such *necessary* things as I found I most *wanted*, particularly a chair and a table; for without these I was not able to *enjoy* the few *comforts* I had in the world; I could not write or eat, or do several things, with so much *pleasure* without a table.'[70] From 'necessary' to 'comforts' and 'pleasure', from 'wanted' to 'enjoy' in fifty-six words: a modulation so rapid that it seems to confirm Mandeville's sarcasm, or the OED's non-committal definition of 'necessaries on the one hand, and luxuries on the other'. But if we look at Robinson's *actual* comforts, the notion loses its supposed equidistance: writing, eating, and 'doing several things' with a table are all things clearly inclining towards necessity—and with absolutely no relationship to luxury. Luxury is always somewhat out of the ordinary; comfort, never; whence the profound common sense of its pleasures, so different from luxury's perverse delight in being 'ornate, grotesque, inconvenient . . . to the point of distress', as Veblen ferociously put it in *Theory of the Leisure Class*;[71] less caustic, but just as trenchant, Braudel dismissed *ancien régime* luxury as 'all the more false', because 'it was not always accompanied by what we would call comfort. Heating was still poor, ventilation derisory.'[72]

Comfort, as everyday necessities made pleasant. Within this new horizon, an aspect of the original meaning of the term returns to the surface. 'Relief', 'aid', 'sustenance' from 'want, pain, sickness', the word used to mean. Centuries later, the need for relief has returned: this time though, not relief from sickness but from—work. It's striking how many of the modern comforts address the need that

---

and that of convenience: comfort includes some kind of pleasure, and convenience does not.

70   Defoe, *Robinson Crusoe*, p. 85 (emphasis added).
71   Thorstein Veblen, *Theory of the Leisure Class*, Harmondsworth 1979 (1899), pp. 182–3.
72   Fernand Braudel, *Capitalism and Material Life 1400–1800*, New York 1973 (1967), p. 235.

from work most directly arises: *rest*. (The first comfort that Robinson wishes for—poor man—is a chair.)[73] It is this proximity to work that makes comfort 'permissible' for the Protestant ethic; well-being, yes; but one that doesn't seduce you away from your calling, because it remains too sober and modest to do so. Much too modest, retort some recent historians of capitalism; much too sober to play a significant role in the precipitous changes of modern history. Comfort indicates those desires 'that could be satiated', writes Jan de Vries, and that therefore have in-built limitations; to explain the open-enedness of the 'consumer revolution', and of the later economic take-off, we must turn instead to the 'volatile "daydreams of desire"',[74] or the 'maverick spirit of fashion'[75] first noticed by the economists of Defoe's generation. The eighteenth century, concludes Neil McKendrick, with a formulation that leaves no conceptual room for comfort, is the age when 'the dictate of need' was superseded once and for all by 'the dictate of fashion'.[76]

Fashion instead of comfort, then? In one respect, the alternative is clearly groundless, as both have contributed to shape modern consumer culture. What is true, however, is that they have done so in different ways, and with opposite class connotations. Already active within court society, and preserving to this day a halo of hauteur, and indeed of luxury, fashion appeals to the bourgeoisie

---

73   'Comforts, or conveniences', Cardinal Newman will write, are things 'like an easy chair or a good fire, which do their part in dispelling cold and fatigue, though nature provides both means of rest and animal heat without them.' John Henry Newman, *The Idea of a University*, London 1907 (1852), p. 209.

74   Jan de Vries, *The Industrious Revolution*, pp. 21, 23. De Vries adopts here the—wholly ahistorical—antithesis of comfort and pleasure of Tibor Scitovsky's *The Joyless Economy*, Oxford 1976.

75   Joyce Oldham Appleby, *Economic Thought and Ideology in Seventeenth-Century England*, Los Angeles 2004 (1978), pp. 186, 191.

76   Neil McKendrick, 'Introduction' to Neil McKendrick, John Brewer and J. H. Plumb, *The Birth of a Consumer Society: The Commercialization of Eighteenth-Century England*, Bloomington, IN, 1982, p. 1.

that wants to go beyond itself, and resemble the old ruling class; comfort remains down to earth, prosaic; its aesthetics, if there is such a thing, is understated, functional, adapted to the everyday, and even to work.[77] This makes comfort less visible than fashion, but infinitely more capable of permeating the interstices of existence; a knack for dissemination that it shares with those other typical eighteenth-century commodities—they, too, somewhere in between necessaries and luxuries—that are coffee and tobacco, chocolate and spirits. *Genussmittel*, as the German word goes: 'means of pleasure' (and in that 'means' one hears the unmistakable echo of instrumental reason). 'Stimulants', as they will also be called, with another striking semantic choice: little shocks that punctuate the day and the week with their delights, fulfilling the eminently 'practical function' of securing 'the individual more effectively into his society because they give him pleasure'.[78]

The accomplishment of *Genussmittel*, writes Wolfgang Schivelbusch, 'sounds like a paradox': *Arbeit-im-Genuss*, reads his definition: work,

---

77   This must be what Schumpeter had in mind when he observed that 'the capitalist style of life could be easily—and perhaps most tellingly—described in terms of the genesis of the modern lounge suit' (Schumpeter, *Capitalism, Socialism and Democracy*, p. 126). Originating in country wear, the lounge suit was used both as a business suit and as a sign of generic everyday elegance; its connection with work, however, made it 'unsuitable' for more festive and fashionable occasions.

78   Wolfgang Schivelbusch, *Tastes of Paradise: A Social History of Spices, Stimulants, and Intoxicants*, New York 1992 (1980), p. xiv. Around 1700, 'coffee, sugar and tobacco moved from being exotic products, to medicinal substances', write Maxine Berg and Helen Clifford; and then—second metamorphosis, identical to that of comfort—they turn from 'medicinal substances' into little everyday pleasures. Work, tobacco, and comfort meet seamlessly in a passage where Robinson declares that he was 'never more vain of my own performance . . . than for my being able to make a tobacco-pipe . . . I was exceedingly comforted with it' (Defoe, *Robinson Crusoe*, p. 153). See Maxine Berg and Helen Clifford, eds, *Consumers and Luxury: Consumer Culture in Europe 1650–1850*, Manchester 1999, p. 11.

mixed with pleasure. It's the same paradox as that of comfort, and for the same reason: during the seventeenth and eighteenth century, two equally powerful but completely contradictory sets of values came simultaneously into being: the ascetic imperative of modern production—and the desire for enjoyment of a rising social group. Comfort and *Genussmittel* managed to forge a compromise between these opposite forces. A compromise, not a true solution: the initial contrast was too sharp for that. So, Mandeville was right about the ambiguity of 'comfort'; what he missed, was that ambiguity *was precisely the point* of the term. At times, that is the best that language can do.

6. PROSE I: 'THE RHYTHM OF CONTINUITY'

By foreshadowing Robinson's actions before they occur, I wrote a few pages ago, final clauses structure the relationship between present and future—I do this, *in order to do* that—through the lenses of 'instrumental reason'. Nor is this limited to Robinson's deliberate planning. Here he is, immediately after the shipwreck: the most calamitous and unexpected moment of his entire life. And yet, he walks

> about a furlong from the shore, to see if I could find any fresh water to drink, which I did, to my great joy; and having drank, and put a little tobacco in my mouth to prevent hunger, I went to the tree, and getting up into it, endeavored to place myself so as that if I should sleep I might not fall; and having cut me a short stick, like a truncheon, for my defense, I took up my lodging.[79]

He goes 'to see' if there is water 'to drink'; then he chews tobacco 'to prevent hunger', places himself 'so as' not to fall, and cuts a stick 'for [his] defense'. Short-term teleology everywhere, as if it were a second nature. And then, alongside this forward-leaning grammar of final clauses, a second choice makes its appearance, inclining in the opposite

---

79   Defoe, *Robinson Crusoe*, p. 66.

temporal direction: an extremely rare verb form—the past gerund: 'and having drank . . . and having put . . . and having cut . . .'—which becomes in *Robinson Crusoe* both more frequent and more significant than elsewhere.[80] Here are a few examples from the novel:

> *Having fitted* my mast and sail, and *tried* the boat, I found she would sail very well . . .

> *Having secured* my boat, I took my gun and went on shore . . .

> . . . the wind *having abated* overnight, the sea was calm, and I ventured . . .

> *Having now brought* all my things on shore *and secured* them, I went back to my boat . . .[81]

What is particularly significant, here, is the grammatical 'aspect', as it is called, of the gerund: the fact that, from the perspective of the speaker, Robinson's actions appear fully *completed*; 'perfected', as the technical term has it. The boat is secured, once and for all; his things have been brought on shore, and will remain there. The past has been demarcated; time is no longer a 'flow'; it has been patterned, and, to that extent, mastered. But the same action that is *grammatically* 'perfected' is *narratively* kept open: more often than not, Defoe's sentences take the successful ending of an action (having secured my

---

80   In the 3,500 novels of the Literary Lab, the past gerund occurs 5 times per 10,000 words between 1800 and 1840, drops to 3 occurrences by 1860, and remains at that level until the end of the century. *Robinson*'s frequency (9.3 per 10,000 words) is thus two to three times higher—and possibly more, given Defoe's habit of using a single auxiliary for two distinct verbs ('having drank, and put', 'having mastered . . . and employed', and so on). That said, since the corpus of the Literary Lab is limited to the nineteenth century, its value for a novel published in 1719 is clearly inconclusive.

81   Defoe, *Robinson Crusoe*, pp. 147, 148, 198 (emphases added).

boat . . .), and turn it into the premise for *another* action: I found she would sail . . . I took my gun . . . I ventured. And then, stroke of genius, this second action becomes the premise for a *third one*:

> . . . and *having fed* it, I *ty'd* it as I did before, *to lead* it away . . .

> . . . and *having stowed* my boat very safe, I *went* on shore *to look* about me . . .

> *Having mastered* this difficulty, and *employed* a world of time about it, I *bestirred* myself *to see*, if possible, how to supply two wants.[82]

Past gerund; past tense; infinitive: wonderful three-part sequence. *Zweckrationalität* has learned to transcend the aims that are immediately at hand, and trace a longer temporal arc. The main clause, at the centre, stands out for its action verbs (I bestirred . . . I went . . . I tied . . .), which are the only ones inflected in a finite form. To its left, and in the past, lies the gerund: half verb, half noun, it confers on Robinson's actions a surplus of objectivity, placing them almost outside his person; labour objectified, one is tempted to say. Finally, to the right of the main clause, and in an unspecified (though never too distant) future, lies the final clause, whose infinitive—often doubled, as if to increase its openness—embodies the narrative potentiality of what is to come.

Past–present–future: 'the rhythm of continuity', as Northrop Frye entitles the pages on prose in *Anatomy of Criticism*. Where, interestingly, very little is actually said about continuity, and very much about the *deviations* from it—from the 'quasi-metrical' equilibrium of the 'Ciceronian balancing of clauses', to the 'mannered prose' that 'over-symmetrizes its material', the 'long sentences in the late novels of Henry James' ('not a linear process

---

82   Ibid., pp. 124, 151, 120 (emphases added).

of thought but a simultaneous comprehension'), or, finally, the 'classical style' that produces 'a neutralizing of linear movement'.[83] Curious, this constant slippage from linear continuity to symmetry and simultaneity. And Frye is not alone in this. Lukács, *Theory of the Novel*:

> Only prose can then encompass the suffering and the laurels, the struggle and the crown, [the path and the consecration] with equal power; only its unfettered plasticity and non-rhythmic rigour can, with equal power, embrace the fetters and the freedom, the given heaviness and the conquered lightness of a world henceforth immanently radiant with found meaning.[84]

The concept is complex, but clear: since, for Lukács, 'every form is the resolution of a fundamental dissonance of existence',[85] and since the specific dissonance of the world of the novel is its being 'infinitely large and . . . rich' in both gifts and dangers,[86] the novel needs a medium that is simultaneously 'non-rhythmic' (so as to adjust to the world's heterogeneity), and yet 'rigorous' enough to endow that heterogeneity with some kind of form. And that medium, for Lukács, is prose. The concept is clear. But is the concept the main point, here? *Theory of the Novel* is subtitled 'An Essay'; and for the young Lukács, the essay was the form which had not yet lost its 'undifferentiated unity with science, ethics, and art'.[87] And art. So, let me quote that passage a second time:

---

83 Northrop Frye, *Anatomy of Criticism: Four Essays*, Princeton 1957, pp. 264–8.

84 Lukács, *Theory of the Novel*, p. 58–9. For some reason, the clause I have placed in square brackets was omitted from Anna Bostock's excellent English translation.

85 Ibid., p. 62.

86 Ibid., p. 34.

87 Georg Lukács, 'On the Nature and Form of the Essay', in *Soul and Forms*, Cambridge, MA, 1974 (1911), p. 13.

Only prose can then encompass
the suffering *and* the laurels,
the struggle *and* the crown,
the path *and* the consecration,
with equal power;
only its unfettered plasticity *and* non-rhythmic rigour
can, with equal power, embrace
the fetters *and* the freedom,
the given heaviness *and* the conquered lightness
of a world henceforth immanently radiant with found meaning.

The words are the same. But now, their symmetry has become visible: one balanced antithesis after another (suffering and laurel, fetters and freedom, given heaviness and conquered lightness . . .), sealed by two synonymous verbs ('encompass'—'embrace'), completed by identical adverbial clauses ('encompass *with equal power*'—'*with equal power* embrace'). Semantics and grammar are here completely at odds with each other: one poses the disharmony of prose as historically ineluctable; the other encases it in a neoclassical symmetry. Prose is immortalized, in an anti-prosaic style.[88]

This page is not, as we will see, Lukács's last word on prose; but it certainly throws light, by contrast, on the style of *Robinson Crusoe*. The succession of past gerund, past tense, and infinitival clauses embodies an idea of temporality—'anisotropic': different, according to the direction one takes—that excludes symmetry, and hence

---

88   Symmetry plays a large role in the aesthetic thought of Georg Simmel, who had a profound influence on the young Lukács. 'The foundation of all aesthetic treatment is to be found in symmetry', writes Simmel in 'Soziologische Aesthetik': 'to give sense and harmony to things, one must first of all shape them in symmetrical fashion, harmonizing the parts into the whole, and ordering them around a central point.' See Georg Simmel, 'Soziologische Aesthetik', *Die Zukunft*, 1896; I am quoting from an Italian translation: *Arte e civiltà*, Milan 1976, p. 45.

also the stability (and the kind of beauty) that proceeds from it. Running from the left to the right of the page—from a fully completed past, to a present that is stabilizing in front of our eyes, and a somewhat indefinite future beyond it—this prose is the rhythm, not just of continuity, but of *irreversibility*. The tempo of modernity is a 'frenzy of disappearance', wrote Hegel in the *Phenomenology*; 'all that is solid melts into air', echoed the *Communist Manifesto*. Defoe's rhythm is not as feverish as those; it is measured, steady; but just as resolute in moving ahead without ever turning back. Capitalist accumulation requires a 'forever *renewed*' activity, writes Weber in *The Protestant Ethic*,[89] and Defoe's sentences—where the success of the first action is the stepping stone for *more* action, and then more beyond that—embody precisely this 'method' that endlessly 'renews' past achievements into new beginnings. It's the grammar of prose as *pro-vorsa*, forward-oriented;[90] the grammar of *growth*: 'Having mastered this difficulty, and employed a world of time about it, I bestirred myself to see, if possible, how to supply two wants . . .'[91] *One* difficulty has been overcome; and now *two* new wants can be addressed. Progress: 'the continuous self-justification of the *present*, by means of the *future* that it gives itself, before the *past*, with which it compares itself'.[92]

The style of the useful. Of prose. Of the capitalist spirit. Of modern progress. But is it really *a style*? Formally, yes: it has its unique grammatical concatenation, and its diffuse thematics of instrumental action. But aesthetically? It's the central problem of a stylistics of prose: its careful determination to move steadily onwards, one step

---

89 Weber, *Protestant Ethic*, p. 21.

90 The idea of prose as a 'forward-oriented discourse [*provorsa*]' that 'knows no regular return' found its classical formulation in Heinrich Lausberg's *Elemente der literarischen Rhetorik*, Munich 1967, § 249.

91 Defoe, *Robinson Crusoe*, p. 120.

92 Hans Blumenberg, *The Legitimacy of the Modern Age*, Cambridge, MA, 1983 (1966–76), p. 32 (emphases added).

at a time is, well, *prosaic*. For now, let me leave it at this: prose style, as having less to do with beauty than with—*habitus*:

> Durable, transposable *dispositions*, structured structures predisposed to function as structuring structures, that is, as principles of the generation and structuring of practices and representations which can be objectively 'regulated' and 'regular' without in any way being the product of obedience to rules, objectively adapted to their goals without presupposing a conscious aiming at ends or an express mastery of the operations necessary to attain them . . .[93]

Defoe's three-clause sentences are an excellent example of Bourdieu's point: 'structured structures' that have come into being without any plan, by the slow accretion of distinct but compatible elements; and that, once they have reached their full form, 'regulate'—without 'consciously aiming' at doing so—the reader's 'practice and representation' of temporality. And the term 'regulate', here, has a profoundly *productive* meaning: its point is not to repress as *ir*-regular other forms of temporal representation, but to provide a template that is at once grammatically tight, yet flexible enough to adapt itself to different situations.[94] Unlike verse, which has 'regulated' educational practices for millennia through a

---

93   Pierre Bourdieu, *Outline of a Theory of Practice*, Cambridge 2012 (1972), p. 72.

94   Aside from the doubling of one, or more, of the three component clauses, *Robinson Crusoe* offers several variations of the basic sequence, by postponing the main clause ('after having laboured hard to find the clay—to dig it, to temper it, to bring it home, and work it—I could not make above two large earthen ugly things (I cannot call them jars) in about two months' labour' [p. 132]), or inserting one more clause in the middle ('Having got my second cargo on shore—though I was fain to open the barrels of powder, and bring them by parcels, for they were too heavy, being large casks—I went to work to make me a little tent with the sail' [p. 73]), or adding other syntactical complications ('the ship having thus struck upon the sand, and sticking too fast for us to expect her getting off, we were in a dreadful condition indeed, and had nothing to do but to think of saving our lives as well as we could' [p. 63]).

mechanism of memorization that demanded *the exact repetition* of
the given structures, prose asks for a *subjective re-production* of
structures that should be similar, yes, but emphatically *not* the same
as the original ones. In *Theory of the Novel*, Lukács found the perfect
metaphor for this: productivity of the spirit.

7. PROSE II: 'WE HAVE DISCOVERED THE PRODUCTIVITY OF THE SPIRIT'

Eager to know more about his 'little kingdom', Robinson decides to
circumnavigate the island. First, some rocks stop him, then the
wind gets in his way. He waits for three days, then ventures out
again, but everything goes disastrously wrong—'a great depth of
water . . . a current . . . my paddles signified nothing'—until he
feels sure he will die. 'And now I saw', he concludes, 'how easy it
was for the providence of God to make even the most miserable
condition of mankind worse.'[95]

The providence of God: the allegorical register of the novel. But a
comparison with the inevitable precedent of *Pilgrim's Progress* reveals
how much has changed, in little more than a generation. In Bunyan,
the allegorical potential of the text was systematically and explicitly
activated by the book's *marginalia*, which transformed the story of
Christian's journey into a *second* text, wherein lay the true meaning of
the book: when Pliable complains about the slow pace of the journey,
for instance, Bunyan's *addendum*—'It is not enough to be *Pliable*'—
turns the episode into an ethical lesson that can be abstracted from the
narrative flow, and preserved forever in its present tense. The story
has a meaning because it has two, and the second is the important one:
this is how allegory works. But *Robinson Crusoe* is different. One of
the humblest words in the English language—'things'—will clarify
what I mean. 'Things' is the third most frequent noun in Bunyan

---

95   Defoe, *Robinson Crusoe*, p. 148.

(after 'way' and 'man'), and the tenth in Defoe (after 'time', and a cluster of terms related to the sea and the island); at first sight, it seems to signal the proximity between the two books, and their distance from the others.[96] But if one looks at the concordances of the term, the picture changes. Here is Bunyan:

All things in parables despise not we . . .

And he makes base things usher in Divine.

. . . to know and unfold dark things to sinners . . .

. . . it is not best to covet things that are now, but to wait for things to come.

. . . for the things which are seen are Temporal; but the things which are not seen are Eternal.

. . . for what things so worthy of the use of the tongue and mouth of men on earth as are the things of the God of heaven?

I am only for setting things right.

Things deep, things hid, and that mysterious be.

. . . to what end should he . . . fill his mind with empty things?[97]

---

96 In *Pilgrim's Progress*, 'things' occurs 25 times every 10,000 words, and in *Robinson* 12; in the late seventeenth and early eighteenth centuries, the average frequency in the Google Books corpus is about ten times lower (between 1.5 and 2.5 every 10,000 words); in the Literary Lab corpus it rises very slowly from 2 occurrences around 1780 to just over 5 in the 1890s.

97 Bunyan, *Pilgrim's Progress*, pp. 7, 9, 26, 28, 60, 65, 95, 100.

In these examples, 'things' possesses three distinct, though partially overlapping meanings. The first is completely generic: 'things' is used to signify insignificance: 'Christian and Faithful told him of all things that had happened to them in the way';[98] 'I am only for setting things right'. The word evokes the 'world' (another very frequent noun, in *Pilgrim's Progress*), and shrugs it off as inessential. Then, another group of expressions—'base things', 'empty things'—adds a second semantic layer, expressing ethical contempt for these insignificant things of the world. And finally, after insignificance and immorality, comes the third incarnation; things become *signs*: 'things in parables', or 'unfold dark things to sinners', or those 'excellent things' that the Interpreter—perfect name—shall explain to Christian during a pause in the journey.

Things that turn into signs; and that can easily do so because, at bottom, *they have never really been things*. In typically allegorical fashion, Bunyan calls forth the world ('things' in meaning one), only to denounce its shallowness (meaning two), and transcend it altogether (meaning three). It's a perfectly logical progression—'from this world to that which is to come', as the full title of *Pilgrim's Progress* has it—where the literal plane is to the allegorical like the body to the soul; it exists only to be consumed, like 'this our City', which, as Christian explains right away, 'I am for certain informed will be burned with fire from Heaven'.[99] Consumed, burned, purified: this is the destiny of things in *Pilgrim's Progress*. And now, *Robinson Crusoe*:

> . . . I had other things which my eye was more upon—as, first, tools . . .

> . . . some of the rigging and sails, and such other things as might come to land . . .

---

98   Ibid., p. 68.
99   Ibid., p. 11.

. . . together with several things belonging to the gunner, particularly two or three iron crows . . .

. . . having no such things as twigs that would bend . . .

. . . the strange multitude of little things necessary in the providing, producing, curing, dressing, making, and finishing this one article of bread.

. . . I could not make above two large earthen ugly things—I cannot call them jars—in about two months' labour.[100]

Here, things are not signs, and certainly neither 'empty' nor 'base'; they are what Robinson 'wants', in the double sense of lack and desire; after all, one of the greatest episodes of the book consists in rescuing a shipload of them from sinking to the bottom of the sea, and being lost forever. The meaning of the term is still generic, inevitably, but this time its indeterminacy encourages a process of specification, rather than a flight from the world: things acquire their meaning, not by ascending 'vertically' onto the plane of eternity, but by flowing 'horizontally' into another clause where they become concrete ('little', 'earthen', 'ugly'), or turn into 'tools', 'iron crows', 'jars', 'twigs that would bend'. They remain stubbornly material, refusing to become signs; like the modern world of *The Legitimacy of the Modern Age*, which is no longer 'responsible for man's salvation', as Bunyan's was, but '*competing* with that salvation with its own offer of stability and reliability'.[101] Stability and reliability: this is the 'meaning' of things in Defoe. It is the 'rise of literal-mindedness' that Peter Burke has dated around the mid seventeenth century,[102] or the parallel shift in Dutch genre painting, 'after

---

100 Defoe, *Robinson Crusoe*, pp. 69, 72, 73, 90, 130, 132.
101 Blumenberg, *Legitimacy of the Modern Age*, p. 47 (emphasis added).
102 Peter Burke, *Varieties of Cultural History*, Cornell 1997, p. 180. See also his earlier article, 'The Rise of Literal-Mindedness', *Common Knowledge* 2 (1993).

1660 or so', from the centrality 'of allegorical devices' to 'the business of everyday life'.[103] 'What grows upon the world is a certain matter-of-factness', will write an unsentimental Victorian: 'a prosaic turn of mind . . . a *literalness*, a tendency to say, "The facts are so-and-so, whatever may be thought or fancied about them."'[104]

The facts are so-and-so. Hegel on prose: 'We may prescribe, as a general rule for prose, literal accuracy, unmistakable definiteness, and clear intelligibility, while what is metaphorical and figurative is always relatively unclear and inaccurate.'[105] So, let's return to the passage mentioned at the beginning of this section, and read it in full:

> The third day, in the morning, the wind having abated overnight, the sea was calm, and I ventured: but I am a warning to all rash and ignorant pilots; for no sooner was I come to the point, when I was not even my boat's length from the shore, but I found myself in a great depth of water, and a current like the sluice of a mill; it carried my boat along with it with such violence that all I could do could not keep her so much as on the edge of it; but I found it hurried me farther and farther out from the eddy, which was on my left hand. There was no wind stirring to help me, and all I could do with my paddles signified nothing: and now I began to give myself over for lost; for as the current was on both sides of the island, I knew in a few leagues distance they must join again, and then I was irrecoverably gone; nor did I see any possibility of avoiding it; so that I had no prospect before me but of perishing, not by the sea, for that was calm enough, but of starving from hunger. I had, indeed, found a tortoise on the shore, as big almost as I could lift, and had tossed it into the boat; and I had a great jar of fresh water, that is to say, one

---

103   Schama, *Embarrassment of Riches*, pp. 452–3.
104   Walter Bagehot, *The English Constitution*, Oxford 2001 (1867), pp. 173–5.
105   Hegel, *Aesthetics*, p. 1005.

of my earthen pots; but what was all this to being driven into the vast ocean . . .'[106]

The day, the morning, the wind which abates—thus causing the sea to calm down. A half-allegorical 'warning' to pilots, then 'accuracy' returns: the point, the boat, the shore, the depth, the current, all the way to the fear of death at the end (with the immediate specification: not by drowning, but starving). Then, more details: he will die of hunger, yes, but he actually has a tortoise on board; a big one, in fact: 'as big as I could lift' (no: *almost* as big); and he has a jar of water, too: a *great* jar of *fresh* water—though it's not *really* a jar, but only 'one of my earthen pots' . . . Unmistakable definiteness. But what is it for? Allegory always had a clear meaning; a 'point'. And these details? There are too many of them, and too insistent, to be the mere 'reality effects'—'insignificant objects, redundant words'—that Barthes will detect in the realist style; still, what are we supposed to do with the fact that Robinson left in the morning, or that the tortoise was as big as it was? The facts are so-and-so. Granted. And they mean—what?

What does the epic epithet mean, asks Emil Staiger in *Basic Concepts of Poetics*—or more precisely: What does the fact that *it is so often repeated* mean? That the sea is *always* the colour of dark wine, and Odysseus full of twists and turns on every day of his life? No; this 'return of the familiar' suggests something more general and much more important: that objects have acquired 'a firm, stable existence', and that, as a consequence, 'life no longer flows on without stopping'.[107] What matters is less the individuality of the given epithet than the *solidity* that its return confers on the epic world. And the same logic holds for the details of literal-minded prose: their significance lies less in their specific content, than in the unprecedented *precision* they

106   Defoe, *Robinson Crusoe*, p. 148.
107   Emil Staiger, *Basic Concepts of Poetics*, University Park, PA 1991 (1946), pp. 102–3.

bring into the world. Detailed description is no longer reserved for exceptional objects, as in the long tradition of *ekphrasis*; it becomes the normal way of looking at the 'things' of this world. Normal, and valuable in itself. It really doesn't make any difference whether Robinson has a jar or an earthen pot; what is important, is the establishment of a mindset that considers details important, *even when they don't immediately matter*. Precision, for precision's sake.

It is at once the most 'natural' and most '*un*-natural' way of observing the world, this unfaltering attention to what is: natural, in that it seems to require no imagination, but only that 'plainness' that has for Defoe 'both in style and method, some suitable analogy to the subject, honesty.'[108] But, also, unnatural: because a page like the one we have read has so many foci of 'local' precision that its overall meaning becomes rapidly hazy. There is a price to pay for precision. 'I have oftentimes . . . delivered things, to make them more clear, in such a multitude of words, that I now seem even to myself to have in divers places been guilty of verbosity', writes the great theorist of 'matters of fact', Robert Boyle, about his way of describing experiments; but, he adds, 'I chose rather to neglect the precepts of rhetoricians, than the mention of those things, which I thought pertinent to my subject, and useful to you, my reader'.[109] A useful verbosity: it could be the formula for *Robinson Crusoe*.

---

108   Daniel Defoe, 'An Essay upon Honesty', in *Serious Reflections during the Life and Surprising Adventures of ROBINSON CRUSOE With his Vision of the Angelic World*, ed. George A. Aitken, London 1895, p. 23.

109   Robert Boyle, 'A Proemial Essay, wherein, with some Considerations touching Experimental Essays in general, Is interwoven such an Introduction to all those written by the Author, as is necessary to be perused for the better understanding of them', in *The Works of the Honourable Robert Boyle*, ed. Thomas Birch, 2nd edn, London 1772, vol. I, pp. 315, 305. In 'The Function of Measurement in Modern Physical Science' (1961), Thomas Kuhn writes about the insistence of the new experimental philosophy 'that all experiments and observations be reported in full and naturalistic detail', and of the fact that 'people like Boyle . . . began for the first time to record their quantitative data, *whether or not they perfectly fit the law*': see Thomas S. Kuhn, *The Essential Tension: Selected Studies in Scientific Tradition and Change*, Chicago, IL, 1977, pp. 222–3.

There is a price to pay for precision. Blumenberg and Lukács expressed it with the same word: totality.

> The strength of the system of the modern age lay in its being oriented towards continued, almost daily confirmations and 'life-worldly' successes of its 'method' . . . its weakness, was its uncertainty what 'totality' this untiring success could ever bring forth.[110]

> Our world has become infinitely large and each of its corners is richer in gifts and dangers than the world of the Greeks, but such wealth cancels out the positive meaning—the totality—upon which their life was based.[111]

The wealth cancels out the totality . . . The point of that page from *Robinson Crusoe* ought to be his sudden terror: he has never been so close to death since the day of the shipwreck. But the elements of the world are so varied, and their accurate mention so demanding, that the general meaning of the episode is constantly deflected and weakened: as soon as our expectations have settled on something, something *else* emerges, in a centrifugal surplus of materials—the corners rich in gifts and dangers—that frustrates all synthesis. Lukács again:

> We have invented the productivity of the spirit: that is why the primeval images have irrevocably lost their objective self-evidence for us, and our thinking follows the endless path of an approximation that is never fully accomplished. We have invented the creation of forms: and that is why everything that falls from our weary and despairing hands must always be incomplete.[112]

---

110 Blumenberg, *Legitimacy of the Modern Age*, p. 473.
111 Lukács, *Theory of the Novel*, p. 34.
112 Ibid., pp. 33–4.

Approximation . . . never accomplished . . . despairing hands . . . incomplete. The world of the *Produktivität des Geistes* is also that 'abandoned by God' of another page of the *Theory* (p. 88). And one wonders: What is the dominant note, here: pride for what has been accomplished—or melancholy for what has been lost? Should modern culture celebrate its 'productivity', or lament its 'approximation'?[113] It's the same question raised by Weber's 'disenchantment' (and Lukács and Weber were very close, in the years of the *Theory of the Novel*); what matters more, in the process of *Entzauberung*: the fact that 'one can, in principle, master all things by calculation'[114]—or that the findings of calculation can no longer 'teach us anything about the *meaning* of the world'?[115]

What matters more? It's impossible to say, because 'calculation' and 'meaning' are for Weber incomparable values, like 'productivity' and 'totality' for Lukács. It's the same fundamental 'irrationality' that we encountered in the bourgeois culture of work a few pages ago: the better prose becomes at multiplying the concrete details that enrich our perception of the world—the better it becomes *at doing its work*—the more elusive is the reason for doing so. Productivity, or meaning. In the following century, the course of bourgeois literature would bifurcate between those who wanted to do the work even better, cost what it may—and those who, faced with the choice between productivity and meaning, decided to choose meaning instead.

---

113   To avoid any misunderstanding: the word 'productivity', in *Theory of the Novel*, does not have the quantitative and profit-oriented meaning current today; it indicates the capacity to produce new forms, rather than merely re-producing 'primeval images'. Nowadays, then, 'creativity' would probably be a better translation than 'productivity'.

114   Weber, 'Science as a Profession', p. 139. *From Max Weber: Essays in Sociology*, edited by H. H. Gerth and C. Wright Mills, Oxford 1958.

115   Ibid., p. 142.

2

Serious Century

I. KEYWORDS IV: 'SERIOUS'

Some years ago, in a book entitled *The Art of Describing*, Svetlana
Alpers observed that—by deciding to 'describe the world seen',
rather than produce 'imitations of significant human actions'—the
painters of the Dutch Golden Age changed forever the course of
European art. In lieu of the great scenes of sacred and profane
history (like the slaughter of the innocents, often mentioned by
Alpers herself), we find still lifes, landscapes, interiors, city views,
portraits, maps . . . In short: 'an art of describing as distinguished
from narrative art'.[1]

It is an elegant thesis; in at least one case, however—the work of
Johannes Vermeer—the real novelty seems to be, not the elimina-
tion of narrative, but the discovery of a *new dimension* of it. Take the
woman in blue, of Figure 4 (following page). What a strange shape
her body has. Is she pregnant, perhaps? And whose letter is she
reading with such concentration? A husband far away, as the map
on the wall suggests? (But if the husband is far away . . .)

---

1 Svetlana Alpers, *The Art of Describing: Dutch Art in the Seventeenth
Century*, Chicago, IL, 1983, pp. xxv, xx.

Figure 4

And the open casket in the foreground: was the letter in there—
is it an *old* letter, then, re-read because there are no recent ones?
(There are so many letters in Vermeer, and they always suggest
a little story: what is being read here and now was written somewhere else, earlier, about even earlier events: three
spatio-temporal layers, on a few inches of canvas). And the
letter in Figure 5, which the servant has just passed on to her
mistress: look at their eyes: worry, irony, doubt, complicity;
you can almost see the servant becoming her mistress's mistress.
And what an odd, oblique frame: the door, the hall, the abandoned mop—is someone waiting for an answer, out on the
street? And in Figure 6, what kind of a smile is that, on the girl's
visage? How much wine has she had, from the pitcher which is
on the table (a real question, in the Dutch culture of the time;

and, again, a narrative one)? What stories has the soldier in the foreground been telling her? And has she *believed* him?

Figure 5

I stop. But a little reluctantly, because all those scenes are indeed, *pace* Alpers, 'significant human actions': scenes from a story, from a narrative. Granted, they are not the great moments of *Weltgeschichte*; but narrative—as the young George Eliot knew perfectly well, including its source in Dutch painting[2]—does not consist only of

2 'I find a source of delicious sympathy in these faithful pictures of a monotonous homely existence, which has been the fate of so many more among my fellow-mortals than the life of pomp or of absolute indigence, of tragic suffering or of world-stirring actions. I turn, without shrinking, from cloud-borne angels, from prophets, sibyls, and heroic warriors, to an old woman bending over her flower-pot, or eating her solitary dinner . . . to that village wedding, kept between four brown walls, where an awkward bridegroom opens

Figure 6

memorable scenes. Roland Barthes, in 'An Introduction to the Structural Analysis of Narrative', found the right conceptual frame for this question, by dividing narrative episodes into the two broad classes of 'cardinal functions' (or 'nuclei'), and 'catalyzers'. Terminology here varies. Chatman in *Story and Discourse* uses 'kernels' and 'satellites'; I will use 'turning points' and 'fillers', mostly for the sake of simplicity. But terminology does not matter, only concepts do. And here is Barthes:

> For a function to be cardinal, it is enough that the action to which it refers open . . . an alternative with consequences for the

---

the dance with a high-shouldered, broad-faced bride, while elderly and middle-aged friends look on . . .': George Eliot, *Adam Bede*, London 1994 (1859), p. 169.

development of the story . . . Between two cardinal functions it is always possible to set out subsidiary notations which cluster around one or the other nucleus without modifying its alternative nature . . . These catalyzers are still functional . . . but their functionality is weak, unilateral, parasitic.[3]

A cardinal function is a turning point in the plot; fillers are what happens *between* one turning point and the next. In *Pride and Prejudice* (1813), Elizabeth and Darcy meet in Chapter 3; he acts contemptuously, and she is disgusted; first action with 'consequences for the development of the story': she is set in opposition to him. Thirty-one chapters later, Darcy proposes to Elizabeth; second turning point: an alternative has been opened. Another twenty-seven chapters, and Elizabeth accepts him: alternative closed, end of the novel. Three turning points: beginning, middle, and ending. Very geometric; very Austen-like. But of course, in between these three scenes Elizabeth and Darcy meet, and talk, and hear, and think about each other, and it's not easy to quantify this type of thing, but, by and large, there seem to be about 110 episodes of this kind. These are the fillers. And Barthes is right, they don't really do much; they enrich and give nuance to the progress of the story, but without modifying what the turning points have established. They are indeed too 'weak and parasitic' to do so; all they have to offer are people who talk, play cards, visit, take walks, read a letter, listen to music, drink a cup of tea . . .

Narration: but of the everyday.[4] This is the secret of fillers.

---

3 Roland Barthes, 'Introduction to the Structural Analysis of Narratives' (1966), in Susan Sontag, ed., *Barthes: Selected Writings*, Glasgow 1983, pp. 265–6.

4 In the early nineteenth century, the semantic field of everydayness— *alltäglich, everyday, quotidien, quotidiano*—drifts towards the colourless realm of the 'habitual', 'ordinary', 'repeatable', and 'frequent', in contrast to the older, more vivid opposition between the everyday and the sacred. To capture this elusive dimension of life was one of Auerbach's aims in *Mimesis*, as is made clear by the book's conceptual leitmotif of the 'serious imitation of the everyday' (*die*

Narration, because these episodes always contain a certain dose of uncertainty (How will Elizabeth react to Darcy's words? Will he agree to walk with the Gardiners?); but the uncertainty remains local and circumscribed, without long-term 'consequences for the development of the story', as Barthes would say. In this respect, fillers function very much like the good manners so dear to nineteenth-century novelists; they are a mechanism designed to keep the 'narrativity' of life under control; to give it a regularity, a 'style'. Here, Vermeer's break with so-called 'genre' painting is crucial; in his scenes, no one is laughing anymore; at most, a smile; but even that, not often. Usually, his figures have the intent, composed face of the woman in blue: serious. Serious, as in the magic formula which defines realism in *Mimesis* (and already for the Goncourts, in the preface to *Germinie Lacerteux*, the novel was *la grande forme sérieuse*). Serious: what is 'in opposition to amusement or pleasure-seeking' (OED); 'in gegensatz von Scherz und Spasz' (Grimm); 'alieno da superficialità e frivolezze' (Battaglia).

But what exactly does 'serious' mean, in literature? 'I have only one question left', we read at the end of the second *Entretien sur le fils naturel* (1757), which introduced the *genre sérieux* into European letters: 'it concerns the genre of your work. It isn't a tragedy; it isn't a comedy. What is it then, and what name should we use for it?'[5] In the opening pages of the third *Entretien*, Diderot responds by defining the new genre as 'intermediate between the two extreme genres', or 'placed in their middle'. It's a great intuition, which

ernste Nachahmung des alltäglichen). Although the title eventually chosen by Auerbach foregrounds the aspect of 'imitation' (*Mimesis*), the book's true originality lies in the other two terms—'serious' and 'everyday'—which had been even more central in the preparatory study 'Über die ernste Nachahmung des alltäglichen' (where Auerbach also considered 'dialectic' and 'existential' as possible alternatives to 'everyday'). See *Travaux du séminaire de philologie romane*, Istanbul 1937, pp. 272–3.

5   Denis Diderot, *Entretiens sur le fils naturel*, in *Oeuvres*, Paris 1951, pp. 1243ff.

Figure 7

updates the age-old connection between style and social class; to the aristocratic heights of tragic passion, and the plebeian depths of comedy, the class in the middle adds a style which is itself in the middle: neither the one nor the other. Neutral; the prose of *Robinson Crusoe*.[6] And yet, Diderot's 'intermediate' form is not quite *equidistant* from the two extremes: the *genre sérieux* 'inclines rather towards tragedy than comedy', he adds,[7] and indeed, as one looks at a masterpiece of bourgeois seriousness like Caillebotte's *Place de l'Europe* (Figure 7), it's impossible not to feel, with Baudelaire, that

---

6   Isn't it curious, muses Dickens in a letter to Walter Savage Landor, in July 1856, 'that one of the most popular books on earth has nothing in it to make anyone laugh or cry? Yet I think, with some confidence, that you never did either over any passage in *Robinson Crusoe*.'

7   Diderot, *Entretiens sur le fils naturel*, p. 1247.

all of its characters 'are attending some funeral or other'.[8] Serious
may not be the same as tragic, true, but it does indicate something
dark, cold, impassable, silent, heavy; an irrevocable detachment
from the 'carnivalesque' of the labouring classes. Serious, is the
bourgeoisie on its way to being the ruling class.

2. FILLERS

Goethe, *Wilhelm Meister's Years of Apprenticeship* (1796); Book II,
Chapter 12. The lovely young actress Philine is flirting with
Wilhelm on a bench in front of the inn; she gets up, walks towards
the hotel, turns back to look at him one last time; after a moment,
Wilhelm follows her—but at the door of the hotel he is stopped by

Melina, the troupe's manager, to whom he has long since promised
a loan. Thinking only of Philine, Wilhelm guarantees the money
for that very evening, and starts to move on; but he is again stopped,
by Friedrich this time, who greets him with his typical warmth . . .
and precedes him upstairs at Philine's. Frustrated, Wilhelm goes to
his room, where he finds Mignon; he is despondent, curt. Mignon is
wounded, Wilhelm doesn't even notice. He goes out again; the
landlord is talking to a stranger, who is looking at him from the
corner of his eye . . .

Hegel's prose of the world: where the individual 'must make
himself a means to others, must subserve their limited aims, and
must likewise reduce others to mere means in order to satisfy his

---

8   Charles Baudelaire, 'The Heroism of Modern Life' (1846), in P. E.
Charvet, ed., *Selected Writings on Art and Artists*, Cambridge 1972, p. 105. In
Fortunata y Jacinta (1887), Pérez Galdós conveys the same diagnosis, but in a
different mood: 'Spanish society began to flatter itself by fancying that it was
"serious", that is to say, it began to dress mournfully: our happy empire of bright
colors was fading away . . . We're under the influence of northern Europe, and
the blasted North imposes on us the grays that it gets from its smoky gray sky . . .'
(Harmondsworth 1986, p. 26).

own interests'.[9] But it's a prose where the bitterness of frustration (Wilhelm, twice held back in his pursuit of pleasure) is curiously mixed with a strong sense of *possibility*. That loan extorted by Melina will launch the theatrical section of the novel, with its memorable discussions of dramatic art; the fear of losing Wilhelm sharpens Mignon's passion (and inspires, a few pages later, the lyrics of *Kennst du das Land*); the stranger at the inn's door is preparing Wilhelm's visit to the castle, where the encounter with Jarno will in turn lead to the Society of the Tower. None of this actually *happens*, in the filler I have described; they are just possibilities. But they are enough to 'reawaken' the everyday, making it feel alive, open; and though its promises will not all be kept (the *Bildungsroman* is also, structurally, the genre of disappointment), that sense of openness will never be totally lost. It is a new, truly *secular* way of imagining the meaning of life: dispersed among countless minute events, precarious, mixed with the indifference or petty egoisms of the world: but also always tenaciously *there*. It's a perspective that Goethe will never seamlessly reconcile with the teleological side of the *Bildungsroman* (plenty of meaning, but all at once, at the end). But the first step has been taken.

Goethe revives the everyday with his sense of possibility; Scott, in *Waverley* (1814), turns to the daily rituals of the past: singing, hunting, eating, toasting, dancing . . . Static scenes, even a little boring; but Waverley is English, he doesn't know what Scottish habits prescribe, asks the wrong questions, misunderstands, insults people—and the routine of the everyday is lit up by small narrative ripples. Not that *Waverley* is as dominated by fillers as *Meister*; the atmosphere is still half Gothic, world history is nigh, stories of love and death create all sorts of melodramatic echoes. But within the melodrama, Scott manages to *slow down* the narrative, multiplying its moments of pause; and within these, he then finds the 'time' to

---

9   G. W. F. Hegel, *Aesthetics*, Oxford 1985 (1823–29), vol. I, p. 149.

develop that analytical style which in its turn generates a new type of description, where the world is observed as if by an 'impartial judge'.[10] Typical of literary evolution, this morphological cascade from fillers to the analytical style, and then to description; interacting with other parts of the structure, the new technique promotes a whole 'wave of gadgets' (as was said of the industrial revolution). A generation, and the gadgets have redesigned the landscape.

Balzac, second book of *Lost Illlusions* (1839): Lucien de Rubempré is (finally!) writing his first article, which will constitute an epoch-making 'revolution in journalism'. It is the chance he has been waiting for since his arrival in Paris. But within this euphoric turning point, a second episode is unconspicuously nested: the newspaper is short of copy; it needs a few pieces, immediately, never mind on what, as long as they fill a few pages; and a friend of Lucien's, obligingly, sits down and writes. It is the Platonic idea of the filler: words written to fill up a blank space, period. But this second article insults a group of characters who, after a long series of twists and turns, will decree Lucien's ruin. It's Balzac's 'butterfly effect': no matter how small the initial event, the ecosystem of the great city is so rich in connections and variables that it magnifies its effects out of all proportion. Between the beginning and the end of an action there is always something that comes in between; some third person who wants to 'satisfy his own interests', as in Hegel's 'prose of world', and deflects the plot in an unforeseeable direction. And so, even the most banal moments of everyday life become like chapters in a novel (which, in Balzac, isn't always a good thing . . .)

The *Bildungsroman*, and the bittersweet mix of frustration and possibility; courtship stories, and the subdued narrativity of manners; the historical novel, and the unexpected rituals of the past; urban multiplots, and the sudden acceleration of life. It is a general

---

10　Walter Scott, *The Heart of Mid-Lothian*, Harmondsworth 1994 (1818), p. 9.

re-awakening of the everyday, that of the early nineteenth century. Then, a generation later, the tide turns. Reflecting on a page where Emma and Charles Bovary are having dinner—could one imagine a more perfect filler?—thus Auerbach:

> Nothing particular happens in the scene, nothing particular has happened just before it. It is a random moment from the regularly recurring hours at which the husband and wife eat together. They are not quarrelling, there is no tangible conflict . . . Nothing happens, but that nothing has become a heavy, oppressive, threatening something.[11]

An oppressive everyday. Because Emma has married a mediocre man? Yes and no. Yes, because Charles is certainly a weight in her life. And no, because even when she is most distant from him—in her two adulteries, with Rudolphe and then with Leon—Emma finds exactly 'the same platitudes of married life', the same 'regularly recurring hours' when nothing significant happens. This collapse of 'adventure' onto banality is even more evident against the background of another novel of adultery—Ernest Feydeau's *Fanny*, of 1858—which at the time was often paired with *Madame Bovary*, but is in fact its polar opposite: a constant oscillation between ecstasis and despair, infamous suspicions and celestial bliss, all conveyed in an implacably hyperbolic manner. Worlds apart from the studious neutrality of *Madame Bovary*, with its heavy, awkward sentences ('they are *things*': Barthes), its 'tone of harmonious grey' (Pater), its '*éternel imparfait*' (Proust). The *imparfait*: the tense that promises no surprises; the tense of repetition, ordinariness, the background—but a background that has

---

11 E. Auerbach, *Mimesis*, Princeton, NJ, 1974 (1946), p. 488. Flaubert's page opens the 1937 essay 'Über die ernste Nachahmung des alltäglichen', which I mentioned earlier; today, when we open *Mimesis*, the first texts we encounter are the *Odyssey* and the Bible; conceptually, though, the book begins with the fillers of *Madame Bovary*, which first gave Auerbach the idea of the 'serious everyday'.

become *more significant than the foreground itself*.[12] A few years later, in *Sentimental Education*, not even the *annus mirabilis* of 1848 can shake the universal inertia: what is truly unforgettable, in the novel, is not the 'unheard-of' of the revolution, but how quickly the waters close down, and the old commonplaces return, the petty egoisms, the weak aimless daydreams . . .

The background, conquering the foreground. The next chapter unfolds in Britain, in a small provincial town that seems ruled by the second law of thermodynamics: imperceptible cooling of generous ardour, writes George Eliot, leading to people 'shapen after the average and fit to be packed by the gross'.[13] In this page, she is reflecting on the young doctor who gave her the fantastic idea of writing the story of a life entirely ruined by—fillers: 'pleasureless yielding to the small solicitations of circumstance, which is a commoner history of perdition than any single momentous bargain'.[14] Sadness; Lydgate doesn't even sell his soul; he loses it in a maze of small events which he does not even recognize *as* events— while they are deciding his life.[15] An unusual young man was

---

12   'Flaubert's novels, and more generally the narrative of realism and naturalism, are marked by a very clear prevalence of the *imparfait* in their narrative sections . . . the background becomes more significant, and the foreground less so': thus Harald Weinrich in his great study *Tempus* (1964, 2nd edn, Stuttgart 1971 [1964], pp. 97–9). Further on, Weinrich adds that the verbal tenses which are typical of the background, and thus also of fillers ('the *imparfait de rupture* in French, and the tenses ending in -*ing* in English'), begin to spread around 1850 (ibid., pp. 141–2). A first look at the 3,500 (English) novels of the Literary Lab supports Weinrich's hypothesis: the past progressive, which occurred around 6 times every 10,000 words in the early part of the nineteenth century, rises to about 11 occurrences by 1860, and 16 by 1880.

13   George Eliot, *Middlemarch*, Harmondsworth 1994 (1872), pp. 144–5.

14   Ibid., pp. 782–3.

15   'Middles and mediations—what the text calls mediums ("unfriendly", "petty", "embroiled", "dim and clogging")—elude the time-killing or merely catalytic function assigned to them, and actually deflect from the ending that they

Lydgate, at his arrival in town; a few years later, he too is 'shapen after the average'. Nothing extraordinary has happened, as Auerbach would say; and yet, everything has.

Finally, in the first year of the new century, the distillation of bourgeois life in Thomas Mann's *Buddenbrooks*: Tom's ironic and dismissive gestures, the judicious words of the Lübeck burghers, Tony's naive excitement, Hanno's painful homework . . . Returning on every page according to the technique of the leitmotif, Mann's fillers lose even the last vestige of a narrative function to become simply—*style*. Everything declines and dies here, as in Wagner, but the words of the leitmotif remain, making Lübeck and its people quietly unforgettable; just like the Buddenbrook family book, where 'respectful significance was granted even to the most modest events'. Words that synthesize beautifully the profound seriousness with which the bourgeois century looked at its daily existence— and which suggest a few further reflections.

3. RATIONALIZATION

What a rapid transition. Around 1800, fillers are still a rarity; a hundred years later they are everywhere (the Goncourts, Zola, Fontane, Maupassant, Gissing, James, Proust . . .). You thought you were reading *Middlemarch*, but no, you were reading a great collection of fillers—which were, after all, the only narrative invention of the entire century. And if such a modest device spread so widely and quickly, there must have been something, in bourgeois Europe, that was eagerly awaiting its appearance. But what? Strange book this *Buddenbrooks*, a reader once wrote to Thomas Mann: so little happens, I should be bored, yet I am not. It *is* strange. How did the everyday manage to become interesting?

---

were meant to reach' (D. A. Miller, *Narrative and Its Discontents*, Princeton 1981, p. 142).

To find an answer, we must do some 'reverse engineering'; reverse, because the solution is given, and we proceed backwards from that to the problem: we know *how* fillers were made, and now we must understand *why* they were made in that way. And in the process, the horizon changes. If we looked for the how of fillers in paintings, novels and narrative theory, their why is outside literature and art, in the realm of bourgeois private life. Beginning, once more, with the Dutch Golden Age, when the private sphere we still inhabit today first found its form; when houses became more comfortable—that word again—and doors multiplied, as did windows, and rooms differentiated their function, with one specializing precisely in everyday life: the 'living', or 'drawing' room (which is actually the '*with*-drawing room', Peter Burke has explained, where the masters withdraw from their servants to enjoy the novelty of 'free time').[16] Vermeer's room, and the novel's: Goethe, Austen, Balzac, Eliot, Mann . . . A protected yet open space, ready to generate a new story with every new day.

But a story intersected by the growing *regularity* of private life. Vermeer's figures are clean, neatly dressed; they have washed their walls, their floors, their windows; they have learned to read, to write, to understand maps, to play the lute and the virginal. They have a lot of free time, yes, but they use it so soberly that it's as if they were always *working*: 'Life is dominated by something that recurs systematically and regularly', writes the young Lukács of *Bürgerlichkeit und l'art pour l'art*,

---

16   Free time is a key precondition 'to participate fully in the values and practices of bourgeois culture', writes Jürgen Kocka in pages that could be describing Vermeer's world: 'one needs a stable income clearly above the minimum . . . the wife and mother as well as the children must be, to some degree, set free from the necessities of work . . . plenty of *space* (functionally specialized rooms in the house or apartment) and *time* for cultural activities and leisure' ('The European Pattern and the German Case', in Jürgen Kocka and Allan Mitchell, eds, *Bourgeois Society in Nineteenth-Century Europe*, Oxford 1993 [1988], p. 7).

by something that happens again and again in obedience to a law, something that must be done without concern for desire or pleasure. In other words, the rule of order over mood, of the permanent over the momentary, of quiet work over genius fed by sensations.[17]

Die Herrschaft der Ordnung über die Stimmung. Weberian shadows. It is Kocka's 'propensity towards regular work and rational life-styles', and the 'hidden rhythms' (Eviatar Zerubavel) of those regularly repeated activities—meals, office schedules, piano lessons, commutes . . . —that bring method into 'the spontaneous character of daily life'.[18] They are the 'good', 'healthy' profits—small but regular, and arising out of a laborious attention to detail—described by Barrington Moore for Victorian Britain;[19] the 'taming of chance' (Ian Hacking) of nineteenth-century statistics, or the irresistible diffusion of words (and deeds) such as 'normalize', 'standardize' . . .[20]

Why fillers, in the nineteenth century? Because they offer *the kind of narrative pleasure compatible with the new regularity of bourgeois life*. They are to story-telling what comforts are to physical pleasure: enjoyment pared down, adapted to the daily activity of reading a novel. 'There has in truth been a great change in the predominant occupations of the ruling part of mankind', writes Walter Bagehot: 'formerly, they passed their time either in exciting action or in

---

17   Georg Lukács, 'The Bourgeois Way of Life and Art for Art's Sake: Theodor Storm', in *Soul and Form*, New York 2010 (1911).

18   Weber, *Protestant Ethic*, p. 154.

19   Barrington Moore, Jr, *Moral Aspects of Economic Growth*, Cornell 1998, p. 39.

20   According to the OED, 'normal', in the sense of 'regular, usual, typical, ordinary, conventional', enters the English language in the late eighteenth century, and becomes common around 1840; 'normalize' and 'standardize' make their appearance a little later, in the second half of the nineteenth century.

inanimate repose. A feudal baron had nothing between war and the chase—keenly animating things both—and what was called "inglorious ease". Modern life is scanty in excitements, but incessant in quiet action.'[21]

Incessant in quiet action: this is how fillers work. There is a profound similarity, here, with the 'rhythm of continuity' we found in Defoe's micro-narrative sequences. In both cases—or better, at both *scales*: the sentence in *Robinson Crusoe*, and the episode in nineteenth-century novels—small things become significant, without ceasing to be 'small'; they become *narrative*, without ceasing to be *everyday*. The diffusion of fillers turns the novel into a 'calm passion', to repeat Hirschmann's great oxymoron for economic interest, or into an aspect of Weber's 'rationalization': a process that begins in the economy and in the administration, but eventually spills over into the sphere of free time, private life, feelings, aesthetics (like the last book of *Economy and Society*, devoted to musical language). Or, finally: fillers *rationalize the novelistic universe*, turning it into a world of few surprises, fewer adventures, and no miracles at all. They are a great bourgeois invention, not because they bring into the novel trade, or industry, or other bourgeois 'realities' (which they don't), but because through them the logic of rationalization pervades *the very rhythm of the novel*. At the height of their influence, even the culture industry falls under their spell: Holmes's armchair 'logic', translating bloody murder into 'a series of lectures'; unbelievable universes, minutely legislated by 'science' fiction; a world best-seller like *Around the World in 80 Days*, devoted to its planetary punctuality, with that hero who lives by train schedules like a Benedectine by his *horarium* . . .[22]

---

21   Walter Bagehot, *The English Constitution*, Oxford 2001 (1867), pp. 173–4.

22   'Punctuality' is of course another typical bourgeois keyword: having indicated for centuries notions like 'precision', 'formality', or 'strictness', it shifted towards 'exact observance of the appointed time' during the nineteenth

But a novel is not just a story. Events and actions, important and not, are conveyed by words; they become language, style. And here, what is happening?

4. PROSE III: REALITY PRINCIPLE

Middlemarch. Dorothea is in Rome, in her room, crying; defence-less, writes Eliot, in front of this 'unintelligible Rome':

> Ruins and basilicas, palaces and colossi, set in the midst of a sordid present, where all that was living and warm-blooded seemed sunk in the deep degeneracy of a superstition divorced from reverence; the dimmer but yet eager Titanic life gazing and struggling on walls and ceilings; the long vistas of white forms whose marble eyes seemed to hold the monotonous light of an alien world: all this vast wreck of ambitious ideals, sensuous and spiritual, mixed confusedly with the signs of breathing forgetfulness and degradation, at first jarred her as with an electric shock, and then urged themselves on her with that ache belonging to a glut of confused ideas which check the flow of emotion.[23]

Eighty-seven polysyllables adding up to form the single gigantic subject of the sentence; and that diminutive 'her' as its only object. The disproportion between Rome and Dorothea could not be better expressed—and in fact, it couldn't be expressed at all without the precision so typical of Eliot's prose style. Ruins and basilicas are 'set' in a present which is 'sordid', and where all that is living (better: 'living and warm-blooded') sinks (no: 'seemed sunk') in a degeneration which is 'deep', and whose 'superstition' is 'divorced from reverence'. Each term is

---

century, when factories and railways, with their fixed schedules, imposed the new meaning with the force of facts.

23   Eliot, *Middlemarch*, p. 193.

observed, measured, qualified, improved. 'I never before longed so much to know the names of things', writes Eliot in her Ilfracombe journal of 1856: 'the desire is part of the tendency that is now constantly growing in me to escape from all vagueness and inaccuracy into the daylight of distinct, vivid ideas'.[24] Escaping from vagueness and inaccuracy; it's a second semantic layer of 'serious': that which 's'applique fortement à son objet', as Littré puts it (and one thinks of Vermeer's woman in blue, with that intent face of a young Mary Ann Evans). 'Seriousness has a well-defined aim', writes Schlegel in the *Athenaeum*, 'hence it can neither idle nor delude itself, but pursues its aim tirelessly until it achieves it.'[25] It's the sense of responsibility of professional ethics; the vocation of the specialist who—like Eliot's narrator, this specialist of language—places herself entirely in the service of the task to be done. And this, as Weber will explain, is not just an *external* duty: the vocation of the modern scientist—and artist—is so 'intimately' entwined to the process of specialization that he becomes convinced 'that the fate of his soul depends upon whether this, and this alone, is the right conjecture to be made . . .'[26] The fate of his soul! And one thinks of the *mot juste*, inevitably, and of Thibaudet's cool assessment of Flaubert's style: 'not a free, prodigious gift, but the product of a discipline which he achieved rather late'.[27] (And Flaubert knew it: 'this book', he wrote to Louis Bouilhet on 5 October 1856, when he saw *Madame Bovary* in print 'shows much more patience than genius—work, more than talent').

---

24   George Eliot, 'Ilfracombe, Recollections, June, 1856', in *George Eliot's Life: As Related in Her Letters*, New York 1903, p. 291.

25   Friedrich Schlegel, *Lucinde and the Fragments*, Minneapolis, MN, 1971, p. 231.

26   Max Weber, 'Science as a Vocation', pp. 135, 137.

27   Albert Thibaudet, *Gustave Flaubert*, Paris 1935 (1922), p. 204.

Work more than talent. This is the nineteenth-century novel. Nor the novel alone. 'Let's take what you call an idea', says the devil in Mann's *Doktor Faustus*:

> a matter of three, four bars, no more, isn't it? All the rest is elaboration, sticking at it. Or isn't it? Good. But now we are all experts, all critics: we note that the idea is nothing new, that it reminds us all too much of something in Rimsky-Korsakov, or Brahms. So, what is to be done? You change it a little. But a changed idea, is that still an idea? Take Beethoven's notebooks! There is no thematic conception there as God gave it. He remolds his theme and adds: 'Meilleur'. Scant confidence in God's prompting, scant respect is expressed in that 'Meilleur'—itself not so very enthusiastic either.[28]

Meilleur. Eliot must have often whispered this word to herself. And one re-reads that page from her great novel and wonders: Was it really worth it? '. . . and then urged themselves on her with that ache belonging to a glut of confused ideas which check the flow of emotion': who can really follow—who can *understand*—these sentences without getting lost in the labyrinth of precision? Remember Defoe: there, the problem with the 'accuracy and definiteness' of prose was that, with the increase in 'local' precision, the overall meaning of the page became opaque: many perspicuous details, adding up to a hazy whole. Here, the problem is radicalized: so strong is Eliot's analytical vocation that *the details themselves* begin to resist understanding. Yet she keeps adding adverbs, participles, subordinates, qualifications. Why? What has made precision so much more important than meaning?

'What advantages accrue to the businessman by double-entry bookkeeping!' reads a famous page from the first book of *Meister*:

---

28 Thomas Mann, *Doktor Faustus*, New York 1971 (1947), p. 237.

This is one of the most beautiful inventions of the human mind, and every serious housekeeper should introduce it into his business . . . Order and clarity increase the desire to save and to acquire. A man who doesn't keep good accounts, who doesn't reckon up what he owes, easily finds himself in a foggy state, whereas [for] a good manager a setback may be an unpleasant surprise, but does not scare him; he can balance this out with the gains he has made elsewhere.[29]

One of the most beautiful inventions . . . For economic reasons, obviously enough, but also, and perhaps even more, for ethical ones: because the precision of double-entry bookkeeping forces people to face facts: all facts, including—and in fact, *especially*—unpleasant ones.[30] The result is what many saw as the moral lesson of science: 'something more mature, more courageous, readier to face unvarnished reality', as Charles Taylor puts it;[31] the maturity of 'manful self-denial, speculation crushed and beguiling illusions willfully destroyed', adds Lorraine Daston.[32] Reality principle.

---

29   Johann Wolfgang Goethe, *Wilhelm Meister's Apprenticeship*, Princeton, NJ, 1995 (1796), p. 18.

30   Exactly what Emma Bovary, that mirror-image of the nineteenth-century bourgeois, will never learn: just before her final ruin, 'now and again . . . she would try to make some calculations; but she would discover such exorbitant things that she could not believe it. She would start again, quickly find herself in a muddle, give it up, and stop thinking about it' (Gustave Flaubert, *Madame Bovary*, Harmondsworth 2003 [1857], p. 234). In her defence, one should remember that, just before becoming the financial myth of the nineteenth century, the Rothschild brothers were exchanging frantic letters on the chaos of their accounts—'In the name of God, such important transactions have to be carried out with precision!'—and wondering whether they were millionaires or bankrupts; 'we are living like drunkards', Mayer Amschel melancholically concluded. See Niall Ferguson, *The House of Rothschild: Money's Prophets 1798–1848*, Harmondsworth 1999, pp. 102–3.

31   Charles Taylor, *A Secular Age*, Cambridge, MA, 2007, p. 365.

32   Lorraine Daston, 'The Moral Economy of Science', *Osiris*, 1995, p. 21. Daston's 'self-denial' is literally inscribed in the historical development of double-entry bookkeeping, from an initial notation quite similar to a journal

With their growing dependence on the market in every aspect of life, write Davidoff and Hall, the middle classes had to learn to keep their income under control, and turned for help to the 'accounting books' provided by the publishing industry, which eventually left their imprint on the rest of their existence: as with that Mary Young who, between 1818 and 1844, next to her house accounts, kept 'a kind of profit and loss ledger of family and social life'—'children's illnesses and inoculations . . . gifts and letters received and given, evenings spent at home . . . calls paid and received . . .'[33]

Third face of seriousness: the *ernste Lebensführung* that was for Mann the cornerstone of bourgeois existence. Beyond ethical gravity, beyond the professional concentration of the specialist, seriousness emerges here as a sort of sublimated commercial honesty—the 'almost religious respect for facts' of the Buddenbrook family book—extended to life as a whole: reliability, method, accuracy, 'order and clarity', *realism*. In the sense, indeed, of the reality principle: where coming to terms with reality becomes, from the necessity it always is, a 'principle'; a value. Containing one's immediate desires is not just repression: it is *culture*. A scene from *Robinson Crusoe*, with its typical alternation of desires (bolded), difficulties (underlined), and solutions (in italics) will give an idea:

The first time I went out I presently discovered that **there were goats in the island, which was a great satisfaction to me**; but then it was attended with this misfortune to me, viz. that they were so shy, so subtile, and so swift of foot, that it was the difficultest thing in the world to come at them. *But I was not discouraged at this*, not doubting but I might now and then shoot one, as it soon happened,

---

entry—where the individuals engaged in the transaction are still flesh-and-blood presences—to the progressive erasure of all marks of concreteness that eventually reduces everything to a series of abstract quantities.

33 Leonore Davidoff and Catherine Hall, *Family Fortunes: Men and Women of the English Middle Class, 1780–1850*, London 1987, p. 384.

for after I had found their haunts a little, I laid wait in this manner for them: *I observed if they saw me in the valleys, tho' they were upon the rocks*, <u>they would run away as in a terrible fright</u>; *but if they were feeding in the valleys, and I was upon the rocks, they took no notice of me, from whence I concluded that by the position of their opticks, their sight was so directed downward, that they did not readily see objects that were above them* . . . The first shot I made among these creatures, I killed a she-goat <u>which had a little kid by her which grieved me heartily</u>; but when the old one fell, the kid stood stock still by her till I came and took her up, and not only so, but when I carry'd the old one with me upon my shoulders, the kid followed me quite to my enclosure, upon which I laid down the dam, and took the kid in my arms, and carried it over my pale, **in hopes to have it bred up tame;** <u>but it would not eat</u>, *so I was forced to kill it and eat it.*[34]

Seven 'but's in a dozen lines. 'Will; tenacious, inflexible, indomitable will is the supreme British quality', writes the *Revue des deux mondes* in 1858, in a piece tellingly entitled 'Du sérieux et du romanesque dans la vie anglaise et américaine'; and this page brimming with adversative clauses—which however don't prevent Robinson from achieving his purpose—abundantly proves the point. Everything is examined *sine ira et studio*, as in Tacitus's maxim with which Weber liked to summarize the process of rationalization; each problem is subdivided into discrete elements (the direction of the goats' eyesight; Robinson's position in the landscape) and solved by a methodical coordination of means and ends. Analytical prose reveals its pragmatic origin, halfway between Bacon's nature (which can be mastered only by being obeyed) and Weber's bureaucracy, with its 'exclusion of love, hatred, and all purely personal, irrational, and emotional elements which escape calculation'. Flaubert: the writer for whom the ' "objective" impersonality'

---

34   Defoe, *Robinson Crusoe*, p. 79.

of the Weberian bureaucrat—'the more perfect, the more he is "dehumanized" '[35]—was the aim of a lifetime.

The more perfect, the more he is dehumanized. There is a sort of ascetic heroism in pursuing this notion—like analytical cubism, serial music, or the *Bauhaus* will do in the early twentieth century. But it's one thing to aim at dehumanized impersonality in an elite avant-garde laboratory, which has its exclusive Faustian rewards; quite another to present it as a general social destiny, like this literature does; in which case, the reality principle of 'speculation crushed' is likely to evoke a painful loss, with no compensation in sight. It's the paradox of bourgeois 'realism': the more radical and clear-sighted its aesthetic achievement—the more unlivable the world it depicts. Could this really be the basis for a broad social hegemony?

5. DESCRIPTION, CONSERVATISM, *REALPOLITIK*

'Objective' impersonality: here is a good synthesis of the analytical style of nineteenth-century novels. Objective, not in the sense that the filter of representation has magically become transparent, of course, but because the subjectivity of the writer has been relegated towards the background. Objectivity increases, *because subjectivity decreases*. 'Objectivity is the suppression of some aspect of the self', write Daston and Galison in *Objectivity*;[36] and Hans Robert Jauss:

> The flourishing historiography of the nineteenth century . . . followed the principle that the historian must efface himself in order for history to be able to tell its own story. The poetics of this method is no different from that of the contemporary peak of literature—the historical novel . . . What so impressed Thierry, Barante, and other

---

35   Max Weber, *Economy and Society*, New York 1968 (1922), vol. III, p. 975.
36   Lorraine Daston and Peter Galison, *Objectivity*, New York 2007, p. 36.

historians of the Twenties, in Scott's novels, was [that] the narrator of the historical novel remains completely in the background.[37]

The narrator in the background. Take *Castle Rackrent*, the 1800 (quasi-)historical novel by Maria Edgeworth, whose work was acknowledged by Scott, in the 1829 *General Preface*, as the model for his own series of novels. *Castle Rackrent* is narrated by an old Irish factotum, Thady Quirk, who allows Edgeworth to create a bridge between past and present, and between the 'here' of her largely English audience and the 'there' of her Irish story. Half abject, half duplicitous, always keen and lively, Thady lends the novel much of its flavour; but certainly not by allowing it 'to tell its own story'. Here is a description from Edgeworth's novel, followed by one from *Kenilworth* (1821), where the presence of the same central object (a Jewish villain, with all the automatic clichés the figure was bound to evoke) rules out a thematic origin for stylistic differences:

> I got the first sight of the bride; for when the carriage door opened, just as she had her foot on the steps, I held the flame full in her face to light her, at which she shut her eyes, but I had a full view of the rest of her, and greatly shocked I was, for by that light she was little better than a blackamoor, and seemed crippled . . .[38]

> The astrologer was a little man, and seemed much advanced in age, for his beard was long and white, and reached over his black doublet down to his silken girdle. His hair was of the same venerable hue. But his eye-brows were as dark as the keen and piercing black eyes which they shaded, and this peculiarity gave a wild and singular cast

37   Hans Robert Jauss, 'History of Art and Pragmatic History', in *Toward an Aesthetic of Reception*, Minneapolis, MN, 1982, p. 55.

38   Maria Edgeworth, *Castle Rackrent* (1800), in *Tales and Novels*, New York 1967 (1893), vol. IV, p. 13.

to the physiognomy of the old man. His cheek was still fresh and ruddy, and the eyes we have mentioned resembled those of a rat, in acuteness, and even fierceness of expression.[39]

In *Castle Rackrent*, Thady intrudes physically in the scene (I got the first sight . . . I held the flame . . . I had a full view), and projects his emotions over the event (*little better than a blackamoor* . . . and *greatly shocked* I was); the point of the passage lies more in conveying his subjective reactions than in introducing a new character as such. In Scott, by contrast, the scene is largely objectified via its physical details: the beard is specified by emotionally neutral adjectives; its length measured against ordinary garments, of which we are told the colour and the material. Here and there, emotional sparks still flicker (a wild cast . . . the eyes resembled those of a rat); but in *Kenilworth*—and although Scott's astrologer is immensely more sinister than Edgeworth's bride—the decisive point is the *analytical presentation* of the character, not its emotional evaluation. Precision; not intensity. So, Jauss is right, in Scott the historian effaces himself, and history is (it appears) telling its own story. But 'story' is not quite right here, because the analytical–impersonal style is much more typical of Scott's *descriptions* than of the narrative proper. And this fact raises another question: What made descriptions so interesting, for nineteenth-century audiences? Fillers were already slowing down the rhythm of the novel; was *another* slowdown really necessary?

The answer, more than in Scott, can be found in Balzac. In Madame Vauquer, writes Auerbach, 'there is no separation of body and clothing, of physical characteristics and moral significance'; more generally, Balzac not only

---

39   Walter Scott, *Kenilworth*, Harmondsworth 1999 (1821), p. 185.

places the human beings whose destiny he is seriously relating in
their precisely defined historical and social setting, but also
conceives this connection as a necessary one: to him every *milieu*
becomes a moral and physical atmosphere which impregnates the
landscape, the dwelling, furniture, implements, clothing, physique,
character, surroundings, ideas, activities, and fates of men . . .[40]

The connection between persons and things conceived 'as a necessary one': the logic of Balzac's descriptions is the same as that of the
most powerful political ideology of his time: conservatism. Adam
Müller 'regards things as extensions of the limbs of the human
body', writes Mannheim, sounding like Auerbach on *Père Goriot*: 'a
fusion of person and thing'; 'a definite, vital, reciprocal relationship'
between owner and property.[41] And the 'fusion' arises from that
other cornerstone of conservatism which is the radical subordination of the present to the past: 'the conservative regards [the present]
simply as *the latest stage reached by the past*',[42] writes Mannheim; and
Auerbach, using almost the same words: 'Balzac conceives the
present . . . as something *resulting from history* . . . people and
atmospheres, contemporary as they may be, are always represented
as phenomena *sprung from historical events and forces*'.[43] In political
philosophy and literary representation alike, the present becomes a
sediment of history; while the past, instead of simply disappearing,

40   Auerbach, *Mimesis*, pp. 471, 473.
41   Karl Mannheim, *Conservatism: A Contribution to the Sociology of Knowledge*,
New York 1986 (1925), pp. 89–90.
42   Mannheim, *Conservatism*, p. 97.
43   Auerbach, *Mimesis*, p. 480. As an example of a character 'resulting from
history', here is a portrait from *Lost Illusions*: '*For thirty years* Jérôme-Nicolas
Séchard had been wearing the famous three-cornered municipal hat *still to be seen*
on the heads of town-criers *in certain provinces*. His waistcoat and trousers were of
greenish velvet. Finally, he wore an *old* brown frock-coat, stockings of patterned
cotton and shoes with silver buckles. This costume, thanks to which *the worker
was still manifest behind the bourgeois*, was . . . so expressive of his way of life, that
he looked as if he had come into the world fully clad' (p. 7; emphasis added).

turns into something visible, solid, *concrete*—to quote another keyword of conservative thought, and of the rhetoric of 'realism'.

Nineteenth-century descriptions became analytical, impersonal, perhaps even 'impartial', as Scott once put it. But the parallel with conservatism suggests that—though this or that individual description may indeed have been relatively neutral—description *as a form* was not neutral at all: its effect was to inscribe the present so deeply into the past that alternatives became simply unimaginable. A new word gave voice to the idea: *Realpolitik*. A politics which 'does not operate within an undefined future, but face to face with what is', wrote Ludwig August von Rochau, who coined the term a few years after the defeat of the 1848 revolutions (more or less at the same time when artistic *réalisme* made its appearance in France). 'Realismus der Stabilität', adds, bitterly, an anonymous liberal observer: the realism of stability and of the *fait accompli*.[44] Not that Balzac is all here, of course; there is also his irrepressible narrative flow, which recalls the paragraphs from the *Communist Manifesto* on the 'everlasting uncertainty and agitation [of] the bourgeois epoch'.[45] But next to Marx's Balzac there is Auerbach's, and this strange mix of capitalist turbulence and conservative persistence suggests something important about nineteenth-century novels (and about literature as a whole): their deepest vocation lies in forging *compromises between different ideological systems*.[46] In our case, the compromise consisted in 'attaching' the two great ideologies of nineteenth-century Europe to different parts of the literary text:

---

44 On von Rochau and the *Grundsätze der Realpolitik*, see Otto Brunner, Werner Conze and Reinhart Koselleck, eds, *Geschichtliche Grundbegriffe*, Stuttgart 1982, vol. IV, p. 359ff. The other quotation (anonymous) can be found in Gerhard Plumpe, ed., *Theorie des bürgerlichen Realismus*, Stuttgart 1985, p. 45.

45 I have discussed at length this aspect of the *Comédie Humaine* in *The Way of the World: The Bildungsroman in European Literature*, London 1987.

46 On literature as compromise formation, the classic study is Francesco Orlando's *Toward a Freudian Theory of Literature*, Baltimore 1978 (1973).

capitalist rationalization reorganized novelistic plot with the regular tempo of fillers—while political conservatism dictated its descriptive pauses, where readers (and critics) increasingly looked for the 'meaning' of the entire story.

Bourgeois existence, and conservative beliefs: such is the foundation of the realist novel, from Goethe to Austen, Scott, Balzac, Flaubert, Mann (Thackeray, the Goncourts, Fontane, James . . .). To this small miracle of equilibrium, free indirect style contributed the final touch.

6. PROSE IV: 'A TRANSPOSITION OF THE OBJECTIVE INTO THE SUBJECTIVE'

Zeitschrift für romanische Philologie, 1887. In the course of a long article on French grammar, the philologist Adolf Tobler observes, in passing, that the presence of the *imparfait* in interrogative sentences is often linked to a 'peculiar mix of indirect and direct discourse, which draws *the verbal tenses and pronouns* from the former, and *the tone and the order of the sentence* from the latter'.[47] The *Mischung* has no name yet, but the decisive intuition has occurred: free indirect style is the meeting ground between two forms of discourse. Here is a passage from one of the first novels to use it in a systematic way:

> The hair was curled, and the maid sent away, and Emma sat down to think and be miserable.—It was a wretched business, indeed!—Such an overthrow of everything she had been wishing for!—Such a development of everything most unwelcome!—Such a blow for Harriet!—That was the worst of all.[48]

---

47   Adolf Tobler, 'Vermischte Beiträge zur französischen Grammatik', *Zeitschrift für romanische Philologie*, 1887, p. 437.

48   Jane Austen, *Emma*, Harmondsworth 1996 (1815), p. 112.

Emma sat down to think *and be miserable*. It was *a wretched business, indeed!* The tone and the order of the sentence, italicized, recall Emma's direct discourse. Emma *sat down* to think and be miserable. It *was* a wretched business, indeed! The tenses, for their part, are those of indirect discourse. And it's strange, one feels simultaneously closer to Emma (because the filter of the narrator's voice is gone), and more distant, because the narrative tenses *objectify* her, thus somehow estranging her from her own self. Here is another example, from the moment in *Pride and Prejudice* when the possibility of a marriage between Darcy and Elizabeth seems irreversibly gone:

> She began now to comprehend that he was exactly the man, who, in disposition and talents, would most suit her. His understanding and temper, though unlike her own, would have answered all her wishes. It was an union that must have been to the advantage of both; by her ease and liveliness, his mind might have been softened, his manners improved, and from his judgment, information, and knowledge of the world, she must have received benefit of greater importance.

As a comment, the words with which Roy Pascal explains Bally's famous article on free indirect style: 'For Bally, simple indirect style tends to obliterate the characteristic personal idiom of the reported speaker; while free indirect style preserves some of its elements—the sentence forms, questions, exclamations, intonations, personal vocabulary, and the subjective perspective of the character.'[49] Preserving the subjective perspective instead of obliterating it: Pascal is discussing language here, but his words could just as well be describing the process of modern socialization—where individual energy is indeed 'preserved', and allowed to express itself, as

---

49   Roy Pascal, *The Dual Voice: Free Indirect Speech and Its Functioning in the Nineteenth-century European Novel*, Manchester 1977, pp. 9–10.

long as it doesn't threaten the stability of social relations. Not for nothing are the two great pioneers of free indirect style—Goethe and Austen—great writers of *Bildungsromane*: the new linguistic device is perfect for granting their protagonists a certain amount of emotional freedom, while simultaneously 'normalizing' them with elements of a supra-personal idiom. 'His understanding and temper, though unlike her own, would have answered all her wishes' . . . who is speaking, here? Elizabeth? Austen?[50] Perhaps, neither one nor the other, but a *third voice*, intermediate and almost neutral among them: the slightly abstract, thoroughly socialized voice of the achieved social contract.[51]

An intermediate, almost neutral voice. Almost. Because, after all, the point of that passage is that Elizabeth is finally seeing her life— 'She *began* now *to comprehend*'—with the eyes of the narrator. She observes herself from the outside, as if she were a third person (a third person: here, grammar is really the message), and agrees with

---

50   'In free indirect style', writes D. A. Miller, 'the two antithetical terms (of character and narration) stand, so to speak, as close as possible to the bar (the virgule, the disciplinary rod) that separates them. Narration comes as near to a character's psychic and linguistic reality as it can get without collapsing into it, and the character does as much of the work of narration as she may without acquiring its authority' (*Jane Austen, or The Secret of Style*, Princeton 2003, p. 59).

51   'With the development of modern fiction', writes Lubomír Dolezel, 'the relationship between [the Discourse of the Narrator and the Discourse of the Character] underwent a dramatic change. In structural terms, this change can be described as a process of "neutralization"' (*Narrative Modes in Czech Literature*, Toronto 1973, pp. 18–19). In the relationship between the narrator's and the character's voice in free indirect style, adds Anne Waldron Neumann, '"neutral" might be more accurate than "sympathetic"', because 'it is not meant to imply the narrator's endorsement, but simply that the two voices do not clash' ('Characterization and Comment in *Pride and Prejudice*: Free Indirect Discourse and "Double-Voiced" Verbs of Speaking, Thinking, and Feeling', *Style*, Fall 1986, p. 390). On free indirect style as a '*third term* between character and narration', and on the '"neutral" accents' of Austen's style, see Miller, *Jane Austen*, pp. 59–60, 100.

Austen. It is a tolerant technique, free indirect style; but it's the technique of *socialization*, not of individuality (not around 1800, at any rate).[52] Elizabeth's subjectivity bows to the 'objective' (that is to say, socially accepted) intelligence of the world: 'une véritable transposition de l'objectif dans le subjectif', as Bally memorably put it a century ago.[53]

We have looked at the beginnings of free indirect style; now, a fully mature example: Emma Bovary, in front of her mirror, after her first act of adultery:

> But when she looked in the mirror, she was startled by her own face. Never had she had eyes so large, so black, so deep. Something subtle, transfiguring, was pervading her person.
>
> She kept saying to herself: 'I have a lover! A lover!', savouring this idea just as if a second puberty had come upon her. At last, she was to know those joys of love, that fever of happiness which she had despaired of. She was entering something marvellous, where everything would be passion, ecstasy, delirium; blue immensity was all about her, the summits of sentiment were glittering in her mind's eye, ordinary appearance appeared only in the distance, far below, in the shadow, in the gaps between these heights.[54]

In February 1857, in his address to the Rouen tribunal, the prosecutor Ernest Pinard reserved for this passage—'much more dangerous, much more immoral than the fall itself'—his most intransigent words.[55] And it makes sense, because those sentences directly

---

52 In the twentieth century, things change; see my sketch in *Graphs, Maps, Trees: Abstract Models for Literary History*, London 2005, pp. 81–91.

53 'Le style indirecte libre en français moderne', *Germanisch-Romanische Monatschrift*, 1912, p. 603.

54 Flaubert, *Madame Bovary*, p. 150–1.

55 'And so, after this first crime, after this first fall, she glorifies adultery, she intones the song of adultery, its poetry, its pleasures. And this, gentlemen, is

contradict 'the old novelistic convention of an always unequivocal moral judgment of the represented characters'.[56] Is there anybody in this novel, Pinard continues,

> who may condemn this woman? No; no one. This is the conclusion. There isn't in the book a single character who may condemn her. If you can find a virtuous character, or even just an abstract principle— one—on whose basis adultery is stigmatized, then I am wrong.

Wrong? No, a century of criticism has fully vindicated him: *Madame Bovary* is the logical endpoint of that slow process which has detached European literature from its didactic functions, replacing an all-wise narrator with large doses of free indirect style.[57] But if the historical trajectory is clear, its meaning is not, and interpretations have gravitated around two incompatible positions. For Jauss (and others), free indirect style places the novel in opposition to the dominant culture, because it forces readers 'into an alienating uncertainty of judgment . . . turning a predecided question of public morals [the evaluation of adultery] back into an open problem'.[58] From this viewpoint, Pinard was right about the stakes of the trial: Flaubert was a threat to the established order. Luckily Pinard lost, and Flaubert won.

---

for me much more dangerous, much more immoral than the fall itself!' (Gustave Flaubert, *Oeuvres*, ed. A. Thibaudet and R. Dumesnil, Paris 1951, vol. I, p. 623).

56 Hans Robert Jauss, 'Literary History as Challenge to Literary Theory' (1967), in *Toward an Aesthetic of Reception*, pp. 43, 632.

57 'In Stendhal and Balzac we frequently and indeed almost constantly hear what the writer thinks of his characters', writes Auerbach in *Mimesis*; 'these things are almost wholly absent from Flaubert's work. His opinion of his characters and events remains unspoken . . . We hear the writer speak; but he expresses no opinion and makes no comment' (p. 486).

58 Jauss, 'Literary History as Challenge to Literary Theory', p. 44. Jauss's thesis is echoed by Dominick La Capra (who writes enthusiastically of Flaubert's 'ideological crime': *Madame Bovary on Trial*, Ithaca, NY, 1982, p. 18), and by the more measured Dorrit Cohn (*The Distinction of Fiction*, Baltimore 1999, pp. 170ff).

The other position reverses the picture. Far from generating uncertainty, free indirect style is a sort of stylistic Panopticon, where the narrator's 'master-voice' disseminates its authority 'by qualifying, canceling, endorsing, subsuming all the other voices it lets speak'.[59] From this second viewpoint, Pinard and Flaubert do not stand for, respectively, repression and critique, but rather for an obsolete and stolid form of social control, and a more flexible and effective one. The trial set them in opposition, true, but deep down they resemble each other much more than they would have admitted; they are *two versions of the same thing*, finally.

By and large, I tend to agree with the latter position, but with one specification. Those sentences from *Madame Bovary* that so exasperated Monsieur Pinard . . . where do they come from? Are they the narrator's words, spoken through Emma's lips? No; they come from the sentimental novels Emma had read as a girl, and never forgotten (the passage continues: 'Then she recalled the heroines of the books she had read . . .'). They are commonplaces, collective myths: signs of the *social* that is inside her. The voice we so often hear in *Pride and Prejudice* is perhaps the 'third voice' of the achieved social contract, I wrote earlier; with Flaubert, we can drop the 'perhaps', because the process has come to its full completion: character and narrator have lost their distinctiveness, subsumed by the composite discourse of bourgeois *doxa*. The emotional tone, the lexicon, the shape of the sentence—all the elements on which we rely to extricate the subjective from the objective side of free indirect style—are now amalgamated in the truly '"objective" impersonality' of the *idée reçue*.

But if this is so, then worrying about the text's 'master-voice' has become superfluous: the control of Emma's soul—'qualifying, canceling, endorsing, subsuming'—is in the hands of the *doxa*,

---

59   D. A. Miller, *The Novel and the Police*, Berkeley, CA, 1988, p. 25.

not of the narrator. In a fully homogenized society, as bourgeois France has become according to Flaubert, free indirect style reveals, not the power of literary techniques, but their *impotence*: its '"objective" seriousness' paralyzes it, making opposition unimaginable; once the entropic drift begins, and the narrator's voice merges with that of the characters (and, through them, of bourgeois *doxa*), there is no way back. Socialization has been *too* successful: from the many voices of the social universe, only 'an average intellectual level' remains, 'around which oscillate the individual intelligences of the bourgeois'.[60] It's the nightmare of *Bouvard and Pécuchet*: no longer knowing how to distinguish a novel about stupidity from a stupid novel.

It is the appropriately bitter epilogue for the serious century of the European novel: a style that, through tireless work, has brought bourgeois prose to an unprecedented level of aesthetic objectivity and consistency—only to discover that it no longer knows what to think about its object. Perfect works, with no *raison d'être*: where, as in *The Protestant Ethic*, 'the irrational sense of having done [one's] job well'[61] is the only tangible—and enigmatic—result. And so, from the centre of capitalist Europe, a warmer, simpler, 'all-too-human' style launches its challenge to bourgeois seriousness.

---

60   René Descharmes, *Autour de 'Bouvard et Pécuchet'*, Paris 1921, p. 65.
61   Weber, *Protestant Ethic*, pp. 70–1.

3

Fog

I. NAKED, SHAMELESS, AND DIRECT

The modern bourgeoisie, reads the famous encomium in the *Communist Manifesto*, 'has accomplished wonders far surpassing Egyptian pyramids, Roman aqueducts, and Gothic cathedrals; it has conducted expeditions . . . agglomerated population, centralized means of production . . . conjured whole peoples out of the ground'.[1] Pyramids, aqueducts, cathedrals, conducted, agglomerated, centralized . . . Clearly, for Marx and Engels, the 'revolutionary role' of the bourgeoisie lies in what this class has *done*. But there is also another, more intangible reason for their praise:

> Wherever it has got the upper hand, the bourgeoisie has put an end to all feudal, patriarchal, idyllic relations. It has pitilessly torn asunder the motley feudal ties that bound man to his 'natural superiors', and has left remaining no other nexus between man and man than naked self-interest, than callous 'cash payment'. It has drowned the most heavenly ecstasies of religious fervour, of chivalrous enthusiasm, of philistine sentimentalism, in the icy

1 Karl Marx and Friedrich Engels, *Manifesto of the Communist Party*, in Robert C. Tucker, ed., *The Marx-Engels Reader*, New York 1978, pp. 338–9.

water of egotistical calculation . . . For exploitation, veiled by religious and political illusions, it has substituted naked, shameless, direct, brutal exploitation.

The bourgeoisie has stripped of its halo every occupation hitherto honoured and looked up to with reverent awe . . . The bourgeoisie has torn away from the family its sentimental veil, and has reduced the family relation to a mere money relation . . . All fixed, fast-frozen relations, with their train of ancient and venerable prejudices and opinions, are swept away, all new formed ones become antiquated before they can ossify. All that is solid melts into air, all that is holy is profaned, and man is at last compelled to face with sober senses his real conditions of life, and his relations with his kind.[2]

Three distinct semantic fields are interwoven in these feverish paragraphs. The first evokes the period that preceded the advent of the bourgeoisie, when the nature of social relations was concealed by a variety of deceptions: a world of 'idylls', 'veils', 'ecstasies', 'enthusiasms', 'holies', 'fervours', 'sentimentalisms', and 'prejudices'. Once in power, however—second passage—the new ruling class has ruthlessly scattered all these shadows: it has 'put an end to idyllic relations', 'torn asunder', 'drowned', 'stripped', 'reduced', 'swept away', and 'profaned'. Whence—finally—the new episteme so typical of the bourgeois age: 'naked self-interest', 'icy calculation', 'sober senses', 'facing one's real conditions', 'naked, shameless, and direct exploitation'. Instead of hiding its rule behind a host of symbolic delusions, the bourgeoisie forces all of society to face the truth about itself. It is the first *realistic* class of human history.

Naked self-interest. The masterpiece of the bourgeois century (Figure 8), 'looks at the viewer', writes T. J. Clark, 'in a way which obliges him to imagine a whole fabric . . . of offers,

---

2   Marx and Engels, *Manifesto of the Communist Party*, pp. 337–8.

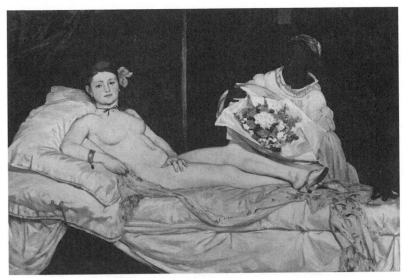

Figure 8

places, payments, particular powers, and status which is still open to negotiation'.[3] Negotiation: the perfect word. Though Olympia is lying down, indolent, and as if doing nothing, she is actually *working*: she has raised her head, and has turned around to assess a potential customer—the viewer of the painting—with that intent gaze that is so hard to hold. Naked, shameless, and direct. Look, by contrast, at Ingres' *Vénus Anadyomène* (1848, Figure 9), with her 'looking which is not quite looking' (Clark again), and the implicit suggestion that 'the nude hides nothing because there is nothing to hide'.[4] It was precisely the 'philistine sentimentalism' of such paint-

---

3   T. J. Clark, *The Painting of Modern Life: Paris in the Art of Manet and His Followers*, London 1984, p. 133.

4   The words, by Camille Lemonnier, are quoted by Clark, *The Painting of Modern Life*, p. 129. An anonymous comment on *The Greek Slave*—the most famous erotic sculpture of the century—expresses the same idea: 'The difference between French and Greek art seems to me simply this—the Frenchman pictures a woman as if she had taken off her clothes to be looked at; the Greek represents one who has never known clothes at all, who is naked but not ashamed.' See Alison Smith, *The Victorian Nude: Sexuality, Morality and Art*, Manchester 1996, p. 84.

ings that *Olympia* set out to unmask: unmistakably, Manet's figure is hiding her genitals with her hand. Realism, indeed.

Figure 9

Manet painted *Olympia*, in Paris, in 1863; seven years later, in London, Millais exhibited his own version of the modern nude: *The Knight Errant* (Figure 10). A knight in full armour, next to a naked woman, twisting a colossal sword towards the ground: it takes some imagination to come up with this. The knight's visor is up, but his eyes are drifting away from the woman, as if lost in thought; and he has an odd way of cutting those ropes, almost hiding behind that large tree. With the woman, it is just as strange: if Ingres' Venus was looking nowhere in particular, Millais' figure looks directly away; or more precisely, she has been *made* to look away: because in the original version, quite sensibly, she was turned towards the knight himself (Figure 11). But the reviews were cold, there were whispers of immorality, the painting didn't sell . . . and Millais cut out her torso, and painted a new one. (Then he combed the hair of the original, lowered her eyes, covered her with a blouse, and sold her as a Protestant martyr: Figure 12.

Figure 10

Figure 11 (x-ray of *The Martyr of Solway*)

Figure 12: *The Martyr of Solway*

The unsheathed sword—and the armour's iron cage; the woman's ubiquitous hair[5]—and the averted face. Ambivalence. Millais wants to paint a naked woman; but he also recoils from doing so. And so, he *narrativizes* her nudity: if the woman is without clothes, it's because she has been caught in a story of aggression, resistance, captivity—with rape and death soon to follow, had the knight not arrived in time. The blood on the blade, the dead man on the right, the running figures in the background are all part of this story (as is Millais' saccharine caption: 'The order of the Knight Errant was instituted to protect widows and orphans and to succour maidens in distress'). And he is not the only one to see things this way; other famous Victorian nudes—from Etty's prototypical *Britomart Redeems Faire Amoret* (1833), to Powers's *Greek Slave* (1844), Landseer's *Lady Godiva's Prayer* (1865), and Poynter's *Andromeda* (1869)—convey the same message: nudity is the result of coercion; it is what savages, or bandits, or tyrants, do to women. In *Olympia*, sex was diurnal, business-like. In Victorian nudes, it is doom; darkness; myth; death. What Manet had prosaically undressed is shrouded once more under the veil of legend.

It's the Victorian enigma: *contra* those paragraphs from the *Communist Manifesto*, the most industrialized, urbanized, 'advanced' capitalism of the age *restores* 'fervours' and 'sentimentalism' instead of 'sweeping them away'.

Why?

2. 'Behind the veil'

Why *was* Victorianism? But the English nude is too petty a feat for such a large question. So:

---

5   Hair is usually extravagantly long in the nude, as if to compensate for its absence near the genitals.

And he, shall he,

Man, her last work, who seem'd so fair,
Such splendid purpose in his eyes,
Who roll'd the psalm to wintry skies,
Who built him fanes of fruitless prayer,

Who trusted God was love indeed
And love Creation's final law—
Tho' Nature, red in tooth and claw
With ravine, shriek'd against his creed—

Who loved, who suffer'd countless ills,
Who battled for the True, the Just,
Be blown about the desert dust,
Or seal'd within the iron hills?
        Tennyson, *In Memoriam*, section LVI

Nature, red in tooth and claw: such a spectacular image that it's often taken as a sign of Darwin's impact on English poetry, whereas of course *In Memoriam* (1850) precedes *The Origin of Species* by several years. As spellbinding as the image itself, however, are the grammatical wonders that Tennyson worked to attenuate its impact: embedding it as a concessive and parenthetical aside (– Tho' Nature . . .), within an interrogative sentence that stretches across four stanzas (shall he / . . . / be blown), and is subdivided into six distinct relative clauses (who seem'd . . . who roll'd . . . who built . . .). The Minotaur, in its labyrinth. Poetic intelligence sees mankind's extinction—and buries it within an unfathomable linguistic maze. Much, much better than Millais' knight: syntactical complexity, in lieu of an iron-clad prude. But the underlying desire is the same: *disavowal*. Take the truth that has somehow emerged, and place it in brackets:

... Or seal'd within the iron hills?

No more? A monster then, a dream,
A discord. Dragons of the prime,
That tare each other in their slime,
Were mellow music match'd with him.

O life as futile, then, as frail!
O for thy voice to soothe and bless!
What hope of answer, or redress?
Behind the veil, behind the veil.

Behind the veil. Charlotte Brontë, on reading a book of natural history: 'If this be Truth, well may she guard herself with mysteries, and cover herself with a veil.' Charles Kingsley, writing to his wife: 'Don't speculate, but if you must, don't speculate too much. Beware of pushing arguments to their logical conclusions.'[6] A generation later, little has changed: 'Ibsen discusses evils which we unfortunately know to exist', writes an anonymous reviewer of *Dollhouse*, 'but which it can serve no good purpose to drag into the light of common day.'[7] What is 'unfortunate' here—the fact that certain evils *exist*, or that we are made to *know* that they exist? Almost certainly the latter. Disavowal. And, again, it's not just a squeamish journalist who expresses this reluctance. 'The inner truth is hidden—luckily, luckily', exclaims Marlow in *Heart of Darkness*. Hidden? Colonies are the truth of the metropolis, wrote Sartre of *The Wretched of the Earth*, and indeed—as Marlow journeys deeper into the Congo—the truth about Kurtz and the colonial enterprise

---

6   Brontë and Kingsley are quoted in Houghton's *Victorian Frame of Mind*, which has much to say about the Victorian tactic of 'deliberately ignoring whatever was unpleasant, and pretending it did not exist'. See Walter E. Houghton, *The Victorian Frame of Mind 1830–1870*, New Haven, CT, 1963, pp. 424, 128–9, 413.

7   Review of *Dollhouse*, unsigned, published in *Between the Acts*, 15 June 1889—now in Michael Egan, ed., *Ibsen: The Critical Heritage*, London 1972, p. 106.

does (almost) come to light: 'It was as if a veil had been rent. I saw on that ivory face the expression of sombre pride, of ruthless power, of craven terror . . .'[8] As if a veil had been rent: so often does Conrad foreground the difficulty of seeing, in *Heart of Darkness*,[9] that this should be the long-awaited epiphany. And instead: 'I blew the candle out and left the cabin.' Wonderful, this return to darkness. That lifted veil, Marlow concludes, was something 'I have never seen before, and hope never to see again'.[10]

---

8   Conrad, *Heart of Darkness*, p. 111.

9   The modal 'could see'—which clearly implies the possibility of *not* seeing, especially in a place of 'darkness'—occurs over thirty times in *Heart of Darkness*; more often than in the entire text of *Middlemarch*, which is ten times as long. Conrad's laborious and ubiquitous similes—like a gauzy and radiant fabric . . . like a weary pilgrimage amongst hints . . . like a sluggish beetle crawling . . . like a somber and polished sarcophagus—further strengthen the fundamental opacity of the novella.

10   Though short, *Heart of Darkness* is a compendium of rhetorical ambivalence. The mention of Kurtz's 'unspeakable rites', for instance (where the adjective is itself at once revelatory and reticent), is entirely contained within a digression—'reluctantly gathered', and bracketed by two extenuating 'buts'— from Marlow's detailed description of the other man's journal. Much like Tennyson's placement of the 'tooth and claw' passage in an aside, Marlow's digression *does* (almost) include the truth, but it relegates it to a position which downplays its significance: when something is mentioned in a lateral branch of a story, there is the implicit suggestion that it cannot be its main point. The same happens in some of Conrad's great sentences: 'Then I went carefully from post to post with my glass', says Marlow as he approaches Kurtz's river house, 'and I saw my mistake. These round knobs were not ornamental but symbolic; they were expressive and puzzling, striking and disturbing—food for thought and also for the vultures if there had been any looking down from the sky; but at all events for such ants as were industrious enough to ascend the pole. They would have been even more impressive, those heads on the stakes, if their faces had not been turned to the house . . .' (p. 96). Ornamental . . . symbolic . . . expressive . . . puzzling . . . striking . . . disturbing . . . food for thought . . . Seven meditative specifications, whose only point lies in delaying the discovery of the truth; when the vultures appear, they are promptly de-realized by a negative hypothetical ('if there had been'); same for the ants, delimited by that 'industrious enough'. There is a lot of linguistic padding around those heads on the stakes—all the way to the final touch of 'if their faces had not been turned': as if what mattered were not the

To be sure, disavowal was not a British preserve: in *Doña Perfecta*, Pérez Galdós speaks with feline sarcasm of 'the sweet tolerance of this accommodating century, which has invented strange veils of language and deed to cover up what might be disagreeable to the public eye';[11] while one of Verdi's great choral moments has an entire cast react to the revelation of prostitution—an *Olympia* moment, as it were—by passionately demanding its renewed concealment.[12] Unlike the atemporal stage of Italian opera, however, or the retrograde province of Galdós's 'Villahorrenda', mid-century British capitalism *had* prepared the conditions for the bourgeois realism envisioned by the *Manifesto*; and indeed, Tennyson *had* seen Nature red in tooth and claw, and Conrad the shrunken skulls of imperialism. They saw, and they blew the candle out. This self-inflicted blindness, is the foundation of Victorianism.

3. THE GOTHIC, *UN DÉJÀ-LÀ*

In the mid nineteenth century, there is one novelistic genre that is peculiar—for obvious reasons—to English literature: the so-called 'industrial' or 'condition-of-England' novels, which specialize in the conflict between 'masters and men'. But many of these novels also find room for another type of conflict: this time, between different generations of the same bourgeois family. In *Hard Times* (1854), the utilitarian Gradgrind feels betrayed when he discovers that his children like to go to the circus ('I should as soon have expected

---

existence of impaled heads, but their orientation. In conclusion: yes, we are told that the skulls are there: but we are endlessly *distracted* from them, too.

11   Benito Pérez Galdós, *Doña Perfecta*, New York 1960 (1876), p. 23.

12   In the second act of *Traviata*, having called into question Violetta's identity ('Questa donna conoscete?'), Alfredo throws a bag of money at her feet ('A testimon vi chiamo / Che qui pagata io l'ho!'), thus revealing the prostitute as the truth of the 'courtisane'. But his act arouses such universal indignation— 'Dov'è mio figlio? Io piu' nol vedo'; 'Di sprezzo degno se stesso rende'; 'Alfredo, Alfredo, di questo core'—that the outcome of the scene is an even deeper disguising of the truth.

them reading poetry'); in *North and South* (1855), old Mrs Thornton thunders against the classics ('Classics may do very well for men who loiter away their lives in the country or in colleges'), while her son, a mill-owner, first studies them, and then marries his teacher's daughter; while in Craik's *John Halifax, Gentleman* (1856), the young industrialist Halifax clashes bitterly with his mentor Fletcher, who refuses to disregard his profit in times of widespread famine. The details vary, but the pattern remains consistent: as the two generations are pitted against each other, *the older one turns out to be much more bourgeois than the younger;* sterner, narrower, profit-driven; but also independent, uncompromising, impatient of pre-industrial values; 'too proud to be a gentleman', as was said of Cobden. Except that, here, independence is rewritten as loneliness: Mrs Thornton is a widow, as are Fletcher, Gradgrind, Dombey (in *Dombey and Son* [1848], Millbank (in Disraeli's *Coningsby* [1844]); all marked by a mutilation that has never healed, and that haunts, in one way or another, the lives of their children: in *Dombey and Son* little Paul dies for 'want of vital power'; Fletcher's son is an invalid, who hates his father's tannery, and whose only fortune is to be under the tutelage of the 'gentleman' Halifax; Millbank's son is saved from certain death by little Lord Coningsby, while Gradgrind's daughter barely avoids adultery, and his son becomes a thief and, for all practical purposes, a murderer. I cannot think of any other genre, short of ancient tragedy, where such a bitter curse binds together two consecutive generations. And the message of the plot is unmistakable: there has been only *one* bourgeois genera-tion—and now it's disappearing, perverted or betrayed by its own children. Its moment is over.

The bourgeois vanishing at the moment of capitalism's triumph. And it's not just a fictional *coup de théâtre*. 'It is one of the paradoxes of cultural history', writes Igor Webb in his study of the Bradford Wool Exchange, 'that in the years between 1850 and the early 1870s, when British architecture turned decisively to the service of industrial capitalism, the prevailing architectural style was the Gothic.'[13] Industrial architecture imitating the Middle Ages: a paradox indeed. But the explanation is actually simple: the Bradford industrialists felt a 'sense of social inferiority and political illegitimacy' which their Gothic Exchange managed to disguise as an 'aristocratic nostalgia for the past'. 'The middle-class acceptance of the gothic style in the 1850s', adds Martin Wiener, 'marked a watershed: the cresting of the new culture of the industrial revolution, and the beginning of a yielding by its new men to the cultural hegemony of the old aristocracy.'[14] Though devoted to 'creative destruction in the economic sphere', concludes Arno Mayer, when the new men entered the sphere of culture they became 'enthusiastic champions of traditional architecture, statuary, painting . . . enveloping their exploits and themselves with historical screens'.[15]

A modernizing world, enveloped in historical screens. Two years after the Reform Act, in a burst of impatience, the Zeitgeist burns the Houses of Parliament to the ground, as if asking for a clear break with the past; and instead, the Gothic revival begins: 'the most important public building' of the only industrial country in the world conceived as a cross between a cathedral and a castle.[16] And so on, for the rest of the century: after the 800-foot-long façade of the Houses of Parliament (not to mention the interior), came the kitsch fantasyland hovering over St Pancras ('the west end of a German cathedral combined with several Flemish town halls'—Kenneth Clark again), and the 50-metre ciborium of the Albert Memorial, where allegorical groups of

---

13   Igor Webb, 'The Bradford Wool Exchange: Industrial Capitalism and the Popularity of the Gothic', *Victorian Studies*, Autumn 1976, p. 45.

14   Martin J. Wiener, *English Culture and the Decline of the Industrial Spirit, 1850–1980*, Cambridge 1981, p. 64

15   Arno Mayer, *The Persistence of the Old Regime: Europe to the Great War*, New York 1981, pp. 4, 191–2.

16   Kenneth Clark, *The Gothic Revival: An Essay in the History of Taste*, Harmondsworth 1962 (1928), p. 93.

Manufacture and Engineering share the canopy with the four Cardinal and the three Theological Virtues. Absurd.

Absurd. Yet, the age of turrets and tabernacles was also the high point of Victorian stability; the Age of Equipoise, as it has been called,[17] when the *tranquillità interna* that Gramsci saw as typical of Great Power hegemony reached its zenith.[18] 'Anderson, Wiener and others locate the moment of cultural and moral collapse of the bourgeoisie in the mid-nineteenth century', write John Seed and Janet Wolff in *The Culture of Capital*; but this, they object, is also the moment 'of the demise of Chartism and the incorporation of the working class . . . It is a coincidence which suggests that more is involved in this mid-century restructuring of class relations than loss of middle-class "nerve".'[19] They are right—but so are Anderson and Wiener: there *was* a retreat of bourgeois values, in mid-century; and there was *also* a hegemonic restructuring of class relations. The two are distinct, yet perfectly compatible. 'Faced with a demand for justification', write Luc Boltanski and Eve Chiappello, developing an insight by Louis Dumont, 'capitalism mobilizes 'already-existing' things (*un 'déjà-là'*) whose legitimacy is guaranteed . . . combining them with the needs of capital accumulation.'[20] They are not talking about Victorianism here, but are describing it just the same: in mid-century, capitalism had become too powerful to remain the exclusive concern of those directly involved in it; it had to make sense *for everybody*, and in this respect it was indeed 'faced with a demand for justification'. But the bourgeois class had too

---

17   W. L. Burn, *The Age of Equipoise: A Study of the Mid-Victorian Generation*, New York 1964.

18   Gramsci, *Quaderni del carcere*, vol. III, p. 1577.

19   John Seed and Janet Wolff, 'Introduction', in Janet Wolff and John Seed, eds, *The Culture of Capital: Art, Power, and the Nineteenth-Century Middle Class*, Manchester 1988, p. 5.

20   Luc Boltanski and Eve Chiappello, *The New Spirit of Capitalism*, London 2005 (1999), p. 20.

little cultural weight to provide it, and a feudal–Christian *déjà-là* was 'mobilized' in its stead, establishing a shared symbolism of the upper classes that made their power much harder to challenge. It's the secret of Victorian hegemony: weaker bourgeois identity—and stronger social control.

4. THE GENTLEMAN

The Gothic as the *déjà-là* that shrouds modern capitalism in 'historical screens'. In architecture, it's clear what that means: you build a train station, and cover it with a transept. And in literature? The closest approximation may be the page on the 'Leaders of Industry' in *Past and Present*:

> No Working World, any more than a Fighting World, can be led on without a noble Chivalry of Work . . . Your gallant battle-hosts and work-hosts, as the others did, will need to be made loyally yours; they must and will be regulated, methodically secured in their just share of conquest under you;—joined with you in veritable brotherhood, sonhood, by quite other and deeper ties than those of temporary day's wages![21]

Being an industrialist is not enough to secure the consent of the workers of England, and to 'make them loyally yours'. 'Battle-hosts' must enter the picture, 'share of conquest', 'Chivalry' . . . In order to establish their hegemony, the new men must look for the *déjà-là* of legitimation in the Fighting Aristocracy. But fighting against what?

> Captains of Industry are the true Fighters, henceforth recognizable as the only true ones: Fighters against Chaos, Necessity, and the Devils and Jötuns . . . God knows, the task will be hard: but no noble task was ever easy . . . Difficult? Yes, it will be difficult. Ye

---

21   Thomas Carlyle, *Past and Present*, Oxford 1960 (1843), pp. 278–80.

have shivered mountains asunder, made the hard iron pliant to you as soft putty: the Forest-giants, Marsh-jötuns bear sheaves of golden grain; Aegir the Sea-demon himself stretches his back for a sleek highway to you, and on Firehorses and Windhorses you career. You are most strong. Thor red-bearded, with his blue sun-eyes, with his cheery heart and strong thunder-hammer, he and you have prevailed. Ye are most strong, ye Sons of the icy North, of the far East,—far marching from your rugged Eastern Wildernesses, hitherward from the grey Dawn of Time![22]

Aegir the Sea-demon? Marsh-jötuns bearing sheaves of grain? Is this the same writer from whom Marx took the icy metaphor of the 'cash nexus'? In a sign of what may happen if one asks too much of the past, the most contemporary of Carlyle's pages—his address to the new ruling class—becomes an archaic aberration, where Thor red-bearded, with his cheery heart, makes the leaders of industry *unrecognizable*, more than legitimate. For better or worse, then, there was no Gothic revival in mainstream Victorian literature, and the nineteenth-century bourgeois underwent a more modest transubstantiation: not a captain—let alone a knight—but only a gentleman.

Published in 1856, at the height of the industrial novel's popularity, Dinah Craik's best-seller *John Halifax, Gentleman* opens with a scene in which the Quaker tanner and mill-owner Fletcher rescues fourteen-year-old Halifax from hunger by offering him a job. Always profoundly grateful to his benefactor, during the famine of 1800 Halifax clashes on his behalf with the town's workers, who have learned that Fletcher has plenty of wheat, and are besieging his house. Since Fletcher is a Quaker, and refuses to call in the soldiers, Halifax steps in, immediately pointing out to the crowd that 'to burn down a gentleman's house is—hanging';[23] then, he lets them

---

22 Ibid., pp. 278, 282–3.
23 Dinah Mulock Craik, *John Halifax, Gentleman*, Buffalo, NY, 2005

'hear the click of his pistol'[24] (which in a later scene he fires into the air[25]). At this point, Halifax is still just an accountant, but he already speaks like a true capitalist: 'it was *his* wheat, not yours. May not a man do what he likes with his own?'[26] Period.

Let's move back in time a few decades. When one looks at 'eighteenth-century crowd action', writes E. P. Thompson, it is clear that the idea 'that prices *ought*, in times of dearth, to be regulated' was not just a 'deeply-felt conviction [of] the men and women in the crowd', but was also 'supported by the wider consensus of the community'.[27] But the last uprisings of the century, including the one mentioned in *Halifax*,

> bring us into different historical territory. The forms of action which we have been examining depended upon a particular set of social relations, a particular equilibrium between paternalist authority and the crowd. This equilibrium was dislodged in the wars, for two reasons. First, the acute anti-Jacobinism of the gentry led to a new fear of any form of popular self-activity . . . Second, repression was legitimized, in the minds of central and of many local authorities, by the triumph of the new ideology of political economy.[28]

The triumph of political economy: it was *his* wheat, not yours. But Halifax is not only that. Having sanctioned the absolute rights of private property with the threat of physical violence, he moves to a completely different register; as the uprising subsides, he opens Fletcher's kitchen to the hungry workers (though he refuses them

---

(1843), p. 116.
  24   Ibid., p. 121.
  25   Ibid., p. 395.
  26   Ibid., p. 118.
  27   E. P. Thompson, 'The Moral Economy of the English Crowd in the Eighteenth Century', *Past and Present* 50 (February 1971), pp. 78, 112.
  28   Ibid., p. 129.

beer); later, he shelters the weavers evicted by the landlord Lord Luxmore, and keeps paying them full wages despite an economic downturn (though, again, 'the old fatal cry of "Down with machinery!"' is promptly met by 'a flash of the master's eye'[29]). That the bread riot should end with the defeated workers intoning 'Hurrah for Abel Fletcher! Hurrah for the Quakers!'[30] is of course preposterous; but it's a hyperbolic answer to a perfectly sensible question: given the conflictual nature of industrial society, what must industrialists *do* to secure their workers' consent?

Halifax's answer is clear: 'if you had come to Fletcher and said, "Master, times are hard, we can't live upon our wages", he might . . . have given you the food you tried to steal',[31] he says during the bread riot; and later, to a group of unemployed workers: 'Why not come to my house and ask honestly for a dinner and a half-crown?'[32] Come to Fletcher, come to my house: what a telling expression. The worker as beggar: knocking on the door of the mansion, and asking, not even for work, but for food and alms. And yet, these are precisely the moments when Halifax is more in control of the workers—more 'hegemonic', as it were. 'Suppose I gave you something to eat', he says at the crucial moment, 'would you listen to me afterwards?';[33] and then, 'looking round with a smile': '"Well, my men, have you had enough to eat?" "Oh, ay!" they all cried. And one added—"Thank the Lord!"'[34]

How can industrialists secure their workers' consent? The novel's answer, in line with the '*déjà-là*' of Boltanski and Chiappello, explains Halifax's hold on the workers with his adoption of pre-capitalist values; specifically, of that 'patriarchal conception of the

29 Craik, *John Halifax, Gentleman*, p. 338.
30 Ibid., p. 122.
31 Ibid., pp. 120–1.
32 Ibid., p. 395.
33 Ibid., p. 119.
34 Ibid., p. 120.

master–servant relation' to which nineteenth-century capitalism gave
'a new lease of life, as the most readily available and adaptable ideological support for the inequality of the wage-labour contract'.[35]
Master and servant: thus begins the metamorphosis of the one-sided
bourgeois into a hegemonic gentleman. The paternalism of the
master, who promises to take care of the workers' entire life—Well,
my men, have you had enough to eat?—in exchange for their well-
disposed docility. But there is a difference, with the paternalism of
Thompson's 'moral economy': the latter was shared by a meaningful
portion of the ruling class, and occasionally even survived in official
documents; though in decline, it was a form of *public policy*. Craik's
paternalism is instead a purely *ethical* choice (as proved by the ubiquitous mention of 'goodness' in contemporary reviews); Halifax
behaves as he does because he is a gentle-man; a Christian; an
Evangelical. It's an important choice, on Craik's part, but a problematic one, too. Important because, in unabashedly superimposing
Christian ethics onto the figure of the industrialist, *Halifax* introduces
a key ingredient—which we will encounter again in the course of this
chapter—in the mosaic of Victorian culture. The more admirably
Halifax behaves, however, *the more atypical of the ruling class he also
becomes*; as, indeed, his countless confrontations with other upper-
class characters amply prove. If ethics had to be part of social
hegemony, a more flexible solution than this immaculate hero had to
be found. And so, the same years as *Halifax*, another industrial novel
shifted the centre of the problem from the moral purity of individual
characters to the specific nature of their relationships.

5. Keywords V: 'Influence'

There is no town in the world, writes Canon Parkinson in *The
Present Condition of the Labouring Poor in Manchester*

---

35 Wood, *The Pristine Culture of Capitalism*, pp. 138–9.

where the distance between the rich and the poor is so great, or the barrier between them so difficult to be crossed. The separation between the different classes, and the consequent ignorance of each other's habits and conditions, are far more complete in this place than in any country of the older nations of Europe, or the agricultural parts of our own kingdom. There is far less personal communication between the master cotton spinner and his workmen . . . than there is between the Duke of Wellington and the humblest labourer on his estate.[36]

Personal communication. 'The most proudly independent man', says the heroine of *North and South*, Margaret Hale, to the mill-owner Thornton, 'depends on those around him for their insensible influence on his character';[37] and in her study of the novel, Catherine Gallagher has singled out precisely this passage to reflect on 'influence' as the book's symbolic fulcrum.[38] Interesting word, 'influence': originating in astrology, where it used to indicate the power of the stars over human events, it acquires in the late eighteenth century the more general meaning of 'capacity of producing effects by insensible or invisible means, without employment of material force or formal authority' (OED). The absence of force and formal authority distinguishes it from power in the strict sense, where both traits are of the essence, and aligns it with Gramscian 'hegemony' instead: a form of dominion where 'insensible or invisible means'—the 'molecular transition' evoked by the entry on 'Hegemony and democracy' in the *Quaderni*[39]—play indeed a decisive role.

---

36 Parkinson, *On the Present Condition of the Labouring Poor in Manchester; with Hints for Improving it*, pp. 12–13.

37 Gaskell, *North and South*, p. 112.

38 Catherine Gallagher, *The Industrial Reformation of English Fiction: Social Discourse and Narrative Form 1832–1867*, Chicago 1988, p. 168.

39 Antonio Gramsci, *Prison Notebooks*, ed. Joseph A. Buttigieg, New York 2007, vol. III, p. 345.

Influence as (an aspect of) hegemony. But what can 'insensible means' and 'molecular transition' concretely mean in a place like Manchester? 'In the village or the small market town', writes Asa Briggs, 'influence' could rely 'upon personal contact', and on the well-established 'power of religion'; but as cities grew, and 'the separation of middle-class and working-class areas [became] more and more marked', its effectiveness was fatally undermined.[40] A town like Manchester had newspapers, which could 'manufacture' (Briggs's metaphor) all sorts of 'opinions'; but compared to the strength of personal contact, opinions remained superficial and unstable.[41] And so, in its attempt to re-create a space for 'influence', *North and South* reverses the historical trend: it opens with a series of episodes in which different 'opinions' are foregrounded—industry and agriculture; classical culture and useful knowledge; masters and men—and prove incapable of preventing a social crisis; and then, after a stunning scene in which an otherwise placid character tears a newspaper to shreds with her teeth,[42] it reverts to the older strategy of 'personal contact' as the only possible solution of the industrial 'problem'. Triangular contact, to be precise: between the industrialist Thornton and Margaret Hale (the 'bourgeoise of culture' who is the novel's mediator); between Margaret and the (ex-)union member Higgins; and finally—restoring Parkinson's 'personal communication between the master cotton spinner and

---

40 Asa Briggs, *Victorian Cities*, Berkeley, CA, 1993 (1968), pp. 63–5.

41 In 'The Natural History of the Newspaper', describing the transformation of the United States from 'a nation of villagers' into one of city-dwellers, Robert Park makes the same point: 'a newspaper cannot do for a community of 1,000,000 inhabitants what the village did spontaneously for itself through the medium of gossip and personal contact'. Robert E. Park, Ernest W. Burgess and Roderick D. McKenzie, *The City*, Chicago 1925, pp. 83–4.

42 'And then, [your father] gave me a wicked newspaper to read, calling our Frederick a "traitor of the blackest dye", "a base, ungrateful disgrace to his profession". Oh! I cannot tell what bad words they did not use. I took the paper in my hands as soon as I had read it—I tore it up to little bits—I tore it—oh! I believe Margaret, I tore it with my teeth' (Gaskell, *North and South*, p. 100).

his workmen'—between Thornton and Higgins. 'No mere institutions, however wise . . . can attach class to class as they should be attached', declares Thornton towards the end of the novel, 'unless [they] bring the individuals of the different classes into actual personal contact. Such intercourse is the very breath of life.'[43] 'And you think they may prevent the recurrence of strikes?' asks his interlocutor, going straight to the point. 'A more hopeful man might imagine that', replies Thornton: 'But I am not a hopeful man . . . My utmost expectation only goes so far as this—that they may render strikes not the bitter, venomous sources of hatred they have hitherto been.'[44] Not the bitter, venomous sources . . . Here is how the narrator describes the new state of affairs:

And thence arose that intercourse, which though it may not have the effect of preventing all future clash of opinion and action, when the occasion arose, would, at any rate, enable both master and man to look upon each other with far more charity and sympathy, and bear with each other more patiently and kindly.[45]

Though it may not . . . would at any rate . . . far more charity . . . more patiently . . . Not easy, stating what 'influence' and 'intercourse' actually *do*. 'Master and man' are still master and man, and their 'future clash' remains perfectly possible; the only differences are

---

43 Ibid., p. 391. Semantically related to 'influence', 'intercourse' is another keyword of *North and South*, and in fact—given that half of its occurrences fall in the final 5 per cent of the book, clustering around the improved relationships between Thornton and the workers—as the keyword of closure. Parkinson, for his part, uses both 'influence' and 'intercourse' throughout his pamphlet, often foreshadowing Gaskell's formulations in the novel: 'Let it become . . . a RULE, not to be deviated from, that the master, or some confidential servant of equal education and influence with the master himself, shall become *personally* acquainted with every workman in his employ . . . It is astonishing how much men are conciliated towards one another simply by becoming personally acquainted' (p. 16).

44 Ibid., p. 391.

45 Ibid., p. 381.

those adverbial clauses—'at any rate', 'with far more charity', 'more patiently and kindly'—that spread a virtuous patina over the harsher reality of social relations. So, Raymond Williams was right in dismissing Gaskell's epilogue as 'what we now call "the improvement of human relations in industry"';[46] but if that is true, it's also worth noticing how *poorly* this ideological resolution works. Such a contorted verb sequence: a narrative past tense (and thence arose)—a negative future conditional (though it may not have the effect)—a past suspended between indicative and subjunctive (when the occasion arose)—and another, doubly hesitant, conditional (would, *at any rate*, enable). We have reached the ideological 'point' of the novel: and the sentence can't make up its mind between the mood of reality and that of mere possibility. 'Once brought face to face, man to man, with an individual of the masses around him', reads another passage on the power of influence, 'and (take notice) out of the character of master and workman, in the first instance, they had each begun to recognize that "we have all of us one human heart".'[47] Here, if possible, the language is even more tortured: an opening in the third person singular ('the masses around *him*'); a switch to a second person imperative ('take notice') apparently—and clumsily—addressed to the reader; then a third person plural ('they had each begun'); and an ending that transforms Wordsworth's lonely country beggar into the collectivity of industrial England ('we have all of us'). Words just refuse to cooperate with Gaskell's politics: if the previous sentence couldn't choose between the real and the possible, this one can't even decide what its *subject* should be—while its tone shifts, erratically, between report, injunction, and sentimentality.

'Imaginary resolution of real contradictions' is Althusser's famous formula for ideology; but these awkward cacophonic periods are the opposite of a resolution. And yet, *North and South* is arguably the most

46 Williams, *Culture & Society*, p. 92.
47 Gaskell, *North and South*, p. 380.

intelligent of the industrial novels, and influence is truly its centre of gravity: its failure in endowing it with an intelligible meaning is thus the sign of a larger difficulty in imagining how an 'intellectual and moral hegemony'—to use another of Gramsci's expressions[48]—may concretely come into being in the new industrial society. In the next section, we will reduce the scale of analysis, and look for the 'invisible means' of its propagation at a truly 'molecular' level.

6. PROSE V: VICTORIAN ADJECTIVES

For a book morbidly keen on practical life, Samuel Smiles's bestseller *Self-Help* (1859) has an odd fixation with—adjectives. Failure, we read in the preface, 'is the *best* discipline of the *true* worker, by stimulating him to *renewed* efforts, evoking his *best* powers . . .'[49] As if Smiles couldn't think of a noun without immediately attaching a qualifier to it: patient purpose, resolute working, steadfast integrity, solid reputation, diligent hand, energetic labourers, strong practical man, untiring perseverance, manly English training, gentle coercion . . .

At first, I thought this was just Smiles's obsession. Then I started seeing crowds of adjectives in every Victorian text I read. Had I stumbled upon the stylistic secret of that age? A grammatical parser went to work on the 3,500 novels of the Stanford Literary Lab, and gave its verdict: No. The Victorians used adjectives just as much as other nineteenth-century writers; the frequency kept cycling gently up and down for a hundred years, within a narrow band ranging from 5.7 to 6.3 per cent (though Smiles *was* higher, above 7 per cent). But if the quantitative hypothesis had been clearly falsified, something else was emerging at the semantic level. Clusters were forming within Smiles's prose: 'strenuous individual application',

48   Gramsci, *Quaderni*, 2010–11.
49   Samuel Smiles, *Self-Help*, Oxford 2008 (1859), p. 4.

'energetic labourers', and 'vigorous effort', for instance, evoked the field of hard physical work: strenuous, energetic, vigorous. Then, at the opposite end of the spectrum, an ethical field materialized in expressions such as '*courageous* spirit', '*upright* character', '*manly* English training', and '*gentle* coercion'. But the type of adjective that gave *Self-Help* its peculiar flavour fell somewhere in between these first two: 'invincible determination', 'patient purpose', 'constant work', 'assiduous application', 'untiring perseverance', 'diligent hand', 'strong practical man' . . . What did these adjectives refer to: work, or ethos? Probably, both at once; as if there were no real difference between the physical and the moral. And in fact, after staring long enough at this large middle group, the previous classification began to blur: was 'strenuous individual application' a practical trait—or a moral one? And didn't that 'manly' English training have eminently practical consequences?

What was going on, with the adjectives of *Self-Help*? Let's move back a century, and consider 'strong' in *Robinson Crusoe*. In the novel, there are a handful of expressions like 'strong ideas' or 'strong inclination', but the word is almost always associated with wholly concrete entities like 'raft', 'current', 'stakes', 'fence', 'limbs', 'dam', 'pale', 'stalk', 'baskets', 'enclosure', or 'fellow'. A century and a half later, *North and South*—a novel of men and machines, where physical strength clearly matters—reverses the pattern: a couple of 'strong and massive frame', or 'strong arms', and dozens of 'strong will', wishes, temptation, pride, effort, objection, feeling, affections, truth, words, or intellectual tastes. In *Self-Help*, strong is most frequently associated with will, followed by inventive faculty, patriotism, instinct, propensity, soul, resolution, common sense, temper, and tolerant minds. *Culture and Anarchy* adds strong inspiration, individualism, belief, aristocratic qualities, sagacity, and taste. Another adjective: 'heavy'. In *Robinson*, aside from a few cases of 'heavy heart', what is heavy are casks, wood, goods, things, grindstone, bough, pestle, boat, bear, and the like. In *Halifax*, we find heavy looks, cares, sighs, burthens, notes, news, misfortunes—many of them, in multiple occurrences; in *North and South*, heavy pressure, pain, moisture of tears, life, trance, and pulses of agony; in *Our Mutual Friend*, frown, eyes, unintelligible something, sighs, charges, disappointment, grudges, and reflections. Finally, let's take 'dark'. In *Robinson*, it indicates absence of light, period. In *North and South* we have dark, dim look, dark places of the heart, dark and sacred recess of her heart, dark cloud over his face, anger, hours, and web of his present fortunes. In *Our Mutual Friend*, dark deep underhanded plotting, attention, sleep, combination, frown, lord, ante-chambers of the present world, smile, business, look, cloud of suspicion, soul, expression, motive, face, transaction and side of the story. In *Middlemarch*, dark ages, period, territories of Pathology, silence, times, flight of evil augury, and closet of his verbal memory.

Other instances could easily be added (hard, fresh, sharp, weak, dry . . .), but the point is clear: in Victorian times, a large group of adjectives that used to indicate physical traits begin to be widely applied to emotional, ethical, intellectual, or even metaphysical states.[50] In the process, the adjectives become metaphorical, and hence acquire the emotional ring that is typical of this trope: if, applied to 'fence' and 'cave', 'strong' and 'dark' indicate robustness and absence of light, applied to 'will' and 'frown' they express a positive or negative verdict—half ethical, half sentimental—on the noun they are attached to. Their meaning has changed; and so, more importantly, has their *nature*: their point is no longer to contribute to the 'literal accuracy, unmistakable definiteness, and clear intelligibility' of Hegel's prose,[51] but to convey a miniature value judgment.[52] Not description, but evaluation.

---

50   Only a large-scale study of English adjectives (impossible here) can establish the exact extent and chronology of this semantic shift; all I can say is that, so far, I haven't encountered anything comparable in quantity or quality to the Victorian case.

51   Hegel, *Aesthetics*, p. 1005.

52   Smiles's preference for the attributive use of adjectives over the

Value judgments, then; but of a very particular kind. In a recent
study, Ryan Heuser and Long Le-Khac have charted in detail the
decline in frequency of the semantic fields of 'abstract values',
'social restraint', 'moral evaluation', and 'sentiment' in nineteenth-
century English novels.[53] When they first presented their results, I
was sceptical: sentiment and moral evaluation becoming *less*
frequent in Victorian times? Impossible. But their evidence was
impeccable. And then, another of their findings explained the riddle:
among the semantic fields whose frequency was rising, there was a
group of adjectives that nearly trebled in the course of the century,
and which fell almost without exception—hard, rough, flat, round,
clear, sharp—within the group I have been describing (and which
had also, as an unpublished chart of the collocations of 'sharp'
revealed the same metaphorical associations: sharp eyes, voice,
glance, pain . . .)

Value judgments, Heuser and Le-Khac's study suggests, took more
than one form in nineteenth-century fiction. A first type, in which the

predicative one is part of this transformation. As Dwight Bolinger has pointed
out, when both choices are equally possible, the attributive position tends to
indicate a permanent and essential characteristic (this is a navigable river), while
the predicative describes a transitory situation (this river is navigable today).
Building on this distinction, Bolinger goes on to observe that, in conjunction with
agentive nouns (singer, worker, liar, loser, etc.), numerous adjectives have a
'literal' meaning in the predicative position (the fighter was clean; the typist was
poor) and a metaphorical–evaluative one in the attributive one (a clean fighter; a
poor typist). Though neither identical to mine nor limited to Victorian times,
these findings are similar enough to suggest interesting possibilities for further
study; see Dwight Bolinger, 'Adjectives in English: Attribution and Predication',
Lingua, 1967, pp. 3–4, 28–9. In his essay on 'The "Récit de Théramène" in
Racine's *Phèdre*' (1948), Leo Spitzer had already noticed, in passing, that 'the
preposed adjective does not describe physical facts but draws moral implications
from the bloodshed'; see Leo Spitzer, *Essays on Seventeenth-Century French
Literature*, ed. David Bellos, Cambridge 2009, p. 232.

53 'Quantitative History of 2,958 Nineteenth-Century British Novels:
The Semantic Cohort Method'—Literary Lab Pamphlet 4, available at litlab.
stanford.edu.

judge was perfectly visible, and the lexicon openly value-laden ('shame', 'virtue', 'principle', 'gentle', 'moral', 'unworthy'), unquestionably declined in the course of the century. But in the meantime, with the rise of 'Victorian adjectives', a second type of judgment had become possible: one that was at once more pervasive (because adjectives are just about everywhere) and much more *indirect*: because adjectives don't quite 'evaluate'—which is an explicit and discursive speech act—but posit a given trait *as belonging to the object itself*. And they are *doubly* indirect, of course, when the judgment takes a metaphorical form, in which factual statement and emotional reaction tend to become inextricable from each other.

Let me do my best to be clear, about the type of 'judgment' expressed by Victorian adjectives. When Gaskell, in *North and South*, writes that 'the expression on her face, always stern, *deepened* into *dark* anger', or Smiles, in *Self-Help*, speaks of Wellington's '*strong* common sense', the text expresses a judgment *for which no actual judge can however be found*. It's as if the world were declaring its meaning all by itself. And then, the words that convey the judgment in question—in our case, 'deepened', 'dark', and 'strong'—possess a *limited* evaluative import: they indicate, respectively, a negative and positive opinion of Mrs Thornton's expression and of Wellington's common sense, but they remain well below the strength of terms like 'unworthy' and 'moral', let alone 'shame' and 'virtue'. Victorian adjectives work with small, unpretentious touches—they can afford to, given how frequently they appear—that accumulate inconspicuously, adding up to a 'mentality' for which no explicit founding statement can ever be found. And a typical trait of this mentality is the fact that moral values are not foregrounded *as such* (as they were in early-nineteenth-century judgments), but remain inextricably mixed with emotions. Take that 'dark' that describes Mrs Thornton in *North and South*: there is a sense of offended principles in the word, and of individual rigidity, and some ugliness, too, and the threat of a sudden explosion; there is an 'objective' side (describing Mrs Thornton's emotional state), and a 'subjective' one (reporting the feelings of the narrator). But the hierarchy of these various factors is left undefined, as well as the border between the objective and the subjective. It's this ethico-emotional mix that constitutes the real 'meaning' of Victorian adjectives.

Victorian adjectives: less ethical clarity, but greater emotional strength; less precision, more meaning. 'The most distinctive feature of modern soul and modern books', writes Nietzsche in the *Genealogy of Morals*, is the 'shamefully *moralized* way of speaking which has gradually made all modern judgments of men and things slimy'.[54] Slimy . . . Too much, perhaps. But that 'moralized way of speaking' is definitely the truth of Victorianism. Moral*ized*, more than moral: the point is less the *content* of the ethical code (an unsurprising mix of Evangelical Christianity, *ancien régime* imaginary, and the work ethic), than its unprecedented *omnipresence*: the fact that, in the Victorian universe, all that is, has *some* moral significance. Not much, perhaps; but never missing. It's this incrustation of value judgments over matters of fact that makes Victorian adjectives so exemplary of the culture as a whole.

And so exemplary, too, of a major turning-point in the history of modern prose. Up to now, through a series of small and large choices—the grammar of irreversibility, the rejection of allegorical significance, the 'verbose' search for accuracy, the 'speculation crushed' of the reality principle, the analytical respect for details, the stern objectivity of free indirect style—bourgeois prose had moved in the general direction of Weberian disenchantment: a striking advance in precision, variety, and consistency—but an advance that could no longer 'teach us anything about the *meaning*

---

54   Friedrich Nietzsche, *The Genealogy of Morals*, ed. Walter Kaufmann, London 1967 (1887), p. 137.

of the world'.[55] Well: Victorian adjectives *are all about meaning*. In their world, all that is, has some moral significance, I just wrote, and I was thinking mostly of 'some' and of 'moral'. But the accent could be easily shifted: with Victorian adjectives, all that is, has some moral *significance*. We may have a hazier idea of what it 'is'—but we certainly know *what it feels like* to encounter it. The re-enchantment of the world has begun, at the most 'molecular' level.

What has made precision more important than meaning, I asked in 'Serious Century'. Here, we should reverse the question: What has made meaning more important than precision? And what happens, once that happens?

7. KEYWORDS VI: 'EARNEST'

Adjectives as inconspicuous vehicles of Victorian values. But there was one of them that wasn't inconspicuous at all. 'To Dr Arnold and his admirers', wrote the *Edinburgh Review* in 1858, reviewing the Rugby novel *Tom Brown's Schooldays* (1857) 'we owe the substitution of the word "earnest" for its predecessor "serious".' Substitution is too strong a word for what actually happened; but there is no doubt that the distance between the two terms decreased dramatically in the central part of the century.[56] Clearly, the Victorians found in 'earnest' something they considered important, and that 'serious' lacked. But what? Mohammed 'was one of those who cannot *but* be in earnest', writes Carlyle in *On Heroes*,

---

55   Weber, 'Science as a Profession', p. 142.
56   In the Google Books corpus, 'serious' is almost twice as frequent as 'earnest' until 1840, when the two terms grow closer, occurring respectively five and four times every 100,000 words; after 1870, the paths diverge again (until eventually, in the twentieth century, 'serious' becomes ten times more frequent than 'earnest'). In the 250 novels of the Chadwyck-Healey database the gap disappears altogether between 1820 and 1845, and the same is true (though about a generation later, in 1840–60) for the larger Literary Lab corpus.

Hero-Worship, and the Heroic in History: one of those 'whom nature
itself has appointed to be *sincere* . . .'[57] Sincerity; that is the key. Not
that 'serious' implies insincerity, of course; but its focus on the
actual consequences of one's actions—Schlegel's 'well-defined aim,
tirelessly pursued'—places sincerity entirely beside the point. For
'earnest', on the other hand, the objective results of an action are
less important than the spirit with which it is done; and 'action' is
not quite right, either, because—if seriousness is indeed action-
oriented and temporary (one becomes serious in order to *do*
something)—'earnest' indicates a more permanent quality: what
one *is*, not what one happens to be doing at a given moment.
Carlyle's Mohammed was *always* in earnest.

Two almost synonymous terms, one of which possesses a moral
component that the other lacks. Forced to share the same narrow
semantic space, 'earnest' and 'serious' amplified their differences,
establishing an antithesis that, as far as I know, exists only in
English,[58] and as a result of which 'serious' lost its neutrality, and

---

57 Thomas Carlyle, *On Heroes, Hero-Worship, and the Heroic in History*,
ed. Michael K. Goldberg, Berkeley, CA, 1993 (1841), p. 47.

58 *John Halifax, Gentleman*, where the two terms occur with more or less
the same frequency, offers a good instance of their semantic polarization: the
'earnest/ness/ly' cluster combines ethics, emotions, sincerity, and passion ('Her
earnest kindness, her active goodness, darting at once to the truth and right of
things, touched the women's hearts . . .' [p. 307]; 'He was also eager and earnest
upon other and higher cares than mere business . . . the factory children . . . the
abolition of slavery . . .' [p. 470]), whereas the 'serious/ness/ly' group is
associated with pain, rage, and danger: 'I found John and his wife in serious, even
painful conversation', writes the narrator, as the two are contemplating the
possibility that one of their visitors might be an adulteress (p. 281); later, when
Halifax's son falls in love with the daughter of an ex-Jacobin, 'Mr Halifax,
speaking in that low tone to which his voice fell in serious displeasure, laid a
heavy hand on the lad's shoulder . . . The mother, terrified, rushed between
them' (pp. 401–2). The same in *North and South*: 'earnest' stands for intense
guileless emotion ('the clear, deep-set, earnest eyes'; 'his earnest yet tender
manner'; 'the fond and earnest look'), whereas serious is all that is unwelcome
and frightening: anxiety, errors, annoyance, apprehension, charge, illness,

became 'bad'.[59] But if the word 'serious' could be exiled to a sort of linguistic Purgatory, the objective 'seriousness' of modern life—reliability, respect for facts, professionalism, clarity, punctuality—remained of course as demanding as ever, and it's here that 'earnest' realized its little semantic miracle: *preserving* the fundamental tonality of bourgeois existence, mostly in the adverbial clause 'in earnest', while *endowing it with a sentimental–ethical significance*. It's the same semantic overdetermination of other Victorian adjectives—but applied to the central aspect of modern society. No wonder that 'earnest' became the shibboleth of Victorian Britain.

Victorian Britain . . . By and large, this notion has gone through two major phases, each lasting about a half-century. The first was mostly concerned—to quote Nietzsche's wonderful invective again—with the 'moralistic mendaciousness' of the Victorians; the second, with the structures of power of their society. Two books by Steven Marcus can stand as the signposts of the two interpretive frames: *The Other Victorians*, in 1966, offering the conclusive, pyrotechnic indictment of Victorian hypocrisy; *Engels, Manchester, and the Working Class*, in 1974, inaugurating the new paradigm, where the category of Victorianism lost its self-evidence, and the very term 'Victorian'—which had been so salient in the early part of the century, from *Eminent Victorians* to *The Victorian Frame of Mind*, *Victorian Cities*, *Victorian People*, and indeed *The Other Victorians*— was replaced in title after title by 'Class', 'Police', 'Body Politic', 'Industrial Reformation', 'Political History', or 'Body Economic'. Victorianism had not quite disappeared, but it had clearly lost its

---

imputation, injury . . .

59   The negative associations of 'serious' persist to this day in American English: in recent years, 'serious' appeared in a Bush State of the Union address in connection with terrorist threats, and the 'serious problem' of America's addiction to oil; in an Obama State of the Union, it was associated with the threats of these 'serious times', and with 'banks that have serious problems'.

conceptual value, surviving only as the chronological label for mid-century capitalism, or power more generally.

In so far as speaking of Victorianism could be a way *not* to speak of capitalism, the work of the last forty years makes sense to me. But, clearly, the point of this chapter is that the concept has still a lot to offer to the critical analysis of power. First, though, we should 'extract' Victorianism from the course of British history, and place it in the comparative context of nineteenth-century bourgeois Europe. This doesn't involve 'exporting' the notion to other countries, as Peter Gay has done in *The Bourgeois Experience*, ending up with the dubious result of a Victorian (half-)Europe. For me, Victorianism remains definitely a British trait; but in the sense of being *the specifically British answer to a common European problematic*. The national peculiarity is preserved, but only as one possible outcome of a historical matrix: and Victorianism becomes a topic for comparatists, just as much as Victorianists.

The peculiarity was of course Britain's pre-eminence within nineteenth-century capitalism, which made Victorianism the first instance of cultural hegemony in modern history. 'For every man there comes the moment', says Mariamne, in Hebbel's great tragedy, 'That he who guides his star allows him / To hold the reins himself. This only is dreadful / That one knows not the moment . . .' For the bourgeois, that critical moment came in mid-nineteenth-century Britain, and the choices made then had a unique weight in undermining the 'realistic' (Marx) or 'disenchanted' (Weber) representations of modernity. Think of the stylistic devices discussed in this chapter: the narrative 'motivation' of sexual desire; the syntactical bracketing of inconvenient truths; the adornment of present might with ancient right; the ethical rewriting of social relations; the metaphorical veil projected by adjectives over reality: so many ways to make the modern world 'meaningful' (or not-meaningless, as the case might be). Meaning, becoming more important than precision—*much* more important. If the early bourgeois had been, loosely speaking, a man of knowledge, the Victorian mix of disavowal and sentimentalism transformed him into a being who feared knowledge and hated it. It is this creature, whom we now have to meet.

8. 'WHO LOVES NOT KNOWLEDGE?'

Tom Brown's Schooldays: the novel chosen by the *Edinburgh Review* for its reflections on 'earnest'. 'Shall I tell him . . . he's sent to school to make himself a good scholar?' wonders Squire Brown, as his son Tom is about to leave for Rugby. 'Well, but he isn't sent to school for that', he corrects himself: 'Greek particles, or the digamma' are not the point; rather, 'if he'll only turn out a brave, helpful, truth-telling Englishman, and a gentleman, and a Christian, that's all I want'.[60] Brave, sincere, a gentleman, and a Christian; that's what Rugby is for. And its headmaster (the real, not the fictional one) agrees: 'what we must look for here', he tells the Older Boys to whom he liked to delegate his authority, 'is, first, religious and moral principle; secondly, gentlemanly conduct; thirdly, intellectual ability'. *Thirdly*, intellectual ability. 'Rather than have [physical science] the principal thing in my son's mind', he adds, in a less guarded moment, 'I would gladly have him think that the sun went round the earth'.[61]

The sun going round the earth. The schoolboy Tom Brown has more common sense than that; still, when at the end of the novel he is asked

---

60 Thomas Hughes, *Tom Brown's Schooldays*, Oxford 1997 (1857), pp. 73–4.
61 Arnold's passages are quoted in Lytton Strachey's *Eminent Victorians*, Oxford 2003 (1918), pp. 149, 153. Asa Briggs quotes another memorable dictum: 'mere intellectual acuteness, divested, as it is in too many cases, of all that is comprehensive and great and good [is] more revolting than the most helpless imbecility, seeming to me almost like the spirit of Mephistopheles'. *Victorian People: A Reassessment of Persons and Themes*, rev. edn, Chicago 1975 (1955), p. 144.

what he wants 'to carry away' from Rugby, he realizes that he has no idea; and then: "'I want to be A1 at cricket and football, and all the other games . . . and to please the Doctor; and I want to carry away just as much Latin and Greek as will take me through Oxford respectably.'"[62] Sports; then the Doctor's approval; last, and least, learning 'just as much' for another perfunctory educational cycle. On at least one thing, therefore, Squire, Doctor, and Boy are in perfect agreement: knowledge is *at the bottom* of the educational hierarchy. It's the first strand of Victorian anti-intellectualism, rooted in the military–Christian worldview of the old elite, and revitalized in mid-century by its most prestigious schools (and, later, by careers in the Empire). But it's not the only force pressuring in that direction. 'How one loves to see . . . this thick-skinned, seemingly opaque, perhaps sulky, almost stupid Man of Practice', writes Carlyle in *Past and Present*, 'pitted against some light adroit Man of Theory';[63] and sure enough it doesn't take long for the almost stupid Man of Practice to put to shame his adroit rival.[64] 'Genius may not be necessary', adds Smiles in a chapter entitled 'Application and Perseverance';[65] as for 'schools, academies, and colleges', they, too, are overrated; far better is 'the life-education daily given in our homes, in the streets, behind counters, in workshops, at the loom and the plough, in counting-homes and manufactories'.[66]

Workshops and looms, instead of schools and academies. 'The industrial revolution owed little to scientific theory', observes Houghton, and as a consequence 'the very success of early

---

62   Hughes, *Tom Brown's Schooldays*, p. 313.
63   Carlyle, *Past and Present*, p. 164.
64   'Of all the Nations in the world', adds Carlyle elsewhere, 'the English are the stupidest in speech, the wisest in action . . . if slowness, what we in our impatience call 'stupidity', be the price of stable equilibrium over unstable, shall we grudge a little slowness?' (pp. 165–8).
65   Smiles, *Self-Help*, p. 90.
66   Ibid., pp. 20–1.

technology, instead of encouraging scientific research, confirmed the anti-intellectualism that is indigenous to the business mind'.[67] Anti-intellectualism is 'the anti-Semitism of the businessman', echoes Richard Hofstadter, who has traced its trajectory from Victorian Britain to the post-war United States.[68] This, however, is no longer the jolly barbarism of Squire Brown, with his Greek particles and the digamma; an industrial society *needs* knowledge; but it only truly needs it *in so far as it's useful*. That word, again: a battle-cry of Victorianism, from the Society for the Diffusion of Useful Knowledge, to the industrialist's words in *North and South* ('any man who can read and write starts fair with me in the amount of really useful knowledge'),[69] Newman's *Idea of a University* ('mental culture is emphatically *useful*'),[70] Bagehot's feline touch on Scott—'no man had a more useful intellect'[71]—and countless others. Following knowledge like a shadow, 'useful' turns it into a tool: no longer an end in itself, knowledge is briskly directed by the adjective towards a predetermined function and a circumscribed horizon. Useful knowledge, or: knowledge without freedom.

This, at the 'prosaic' and popular end of the Victorian spectrum. Now, Tennyson:

> Who loves not Knowledge? Who shall rail
> Against her beauty? May she mix
> With men and prosper! Who shall fix
> Her pillars? Let her work prevail.[72]

67   Houghton, *Victorian Frame of Mind*, pp. 113–14.
68   Richard Hofstadter, *Anti-Intellectualism in American Life*, New York 1963, p. 4.
69   Gaskell, *North and South*, p. 79.
70   Newman, *Idea of a University*, p. 166.
71   Walter Bagehot, 'The Waverley Novels' (1858), in *Literary Studies*, London 1891, vol. II, p. 172.
72   Tennyson, *In Memoriam*, CXIV.

Who loves not Knowledge. Of course. But—

> But on her forehead sits a fire:
> She sets her forward countenance
> And leaps into the future chance,
> Submitting all things to desire.
>
> Half-grown as yet, a child, and vain—
> She cannot fight the fear of death.
> What is she, cut from love and faith,
> But some wild Pallas from the brain
>
> Of Demons? Fiery-hot to burst
> All barriers in her onward race
> For power. Let her know her place;
> She is the second, not the first.[73]

Knowledge, with a capital 'K'. But if it's 'cut' from 'love and faith'—if it is 'divested', as headmaster Thomas Arnold would say, of what is 'great and good'—then 'she' becomes 'half-grown' and 'wild', while 'brain' ('Of Demons': Arnold's 'spirit of Mephistopheles') is made to rhyme with 'vain'. And in a poem where enjambment is rather rare, its three consecutive occurrences[74] so interfere with our grasp of syntax that the upper-class sneer of 'Let her know her place' evinces a sigh of metrical relief. And then, of course, 'She is the second, not the first'. A small difference? 'It makes all the difference in the world whether we put Truth in the first place or in the second', reads the motto placed as epigraph to John Morley's *On Compromise* (1874). The first place signifies autonomy; the second, subordination:

---

73   Ibid.

74   'From the brain / Of Demons'; 'to burst / All barriers'; 'onward race / For power'. Metrico-syntactical instability had emerged, with three more enjambments, immediately after the words 'Who loves not Knowledge': 'rail / Against', 'mix / With men', and 'fix / Her pillars'.

. . . She is the second, not the first.

A higher hand must make her mild,
If all be not in vain; and guide
Her footsteps, moving side by side
With wisdom, like the younger child:

For she is earthly of the mind,
But Wisdom heavenly of the soul.[75]

A higher hand. Poor knowledge. When not forced to be 'useful', it has to be good. Its only consolation: beauty has it worse. In the 20,000 words of *In Memoriam*, 'beauty' occurs—twice. Once in the passage we have just seen, where, as an attribute of knowledge ('Who shall rail / Against her beauty?'), it is itself harnessed to heavenly wisdom; and once here:

My own dim life should teach me this,
That life shall live for evermore,
Else earth is darkness at the core,
And dust and ashes all that is;

This round of green, this orb of flame,
Fantastic beauty; such as lurks
In some wild Poet, when he works
Without a conscience or an aim.[76]

Fantastic beauty. But for Tennyson, the adjective is not the euphoric modifier of today; it is like the 'Fantastical Faith' of Ignorance in *Pilgrim's Progress*: it means delusional, ephemeral, dangerous: something that 'lurks'—lurks!—in 'some wild Poet' (like the 'wild

75 Tennyson, *In Memoriam*, CXIII.
76 Ibid., XXXIV.

Pallas' of section CXIV) working 'without a conscience'. That poet must be the protagonist of the following stanza, which, according to his own son, Tennyson had been inspired to write by 'the cry of "Art for Art's sake"':

> Art for Art's sake! Hail, truest Lord of Hell!
> Hail Genius, Master of the Moral Will!
> 'The filthiest of all paintings painted well
> Is mightier than the purer painted ill!'[77]

The 1850s; the years when *Les Fleurs du Mal* and *Madame Bovary* announce the emergence of that autonomous literary field where a text 'can be beautiful, not only in spite of the aspect in which it is not good, but rather *in that very aspect*';[78] so that, yes, the filthiest of all paintings painted well *is* mightier than the purer painted ill. *Olympia* and the *Knight Errant*; we are back there. And what is true for art, Weber goes on, is true for science, too: where 'something may be true although it is not beautiful and not holy and not good'.[79] True, though *neither* beautiful *nor* holy *nor* good: more than any specific content, it is this radical *separation of the intellectual spheres* that defines the novelty of bourgeois culture, and makes 'Science as a Profession' its great manifesto. Science and art must be neither 'useful' nor 'wise'; they must only follow their inner logic. Autonomy. But autonomy, was precisely what the Victorian manifesto was written against.

---

77   Hallam Tennyson, *Alfred Lord Tennyson: A Memoir by his Son*, New York 1897, p. 92.
78   Max Weber, 'Science as a Profession', p. 147.
79   Ibid., p. 148.

9. PROSE VI: FOG

'Hitherto I have been insisting chiefly on beauty', writes Matthew Arnold, opening the second section of *Culture and Anarchy* (1869).[80] Has he? True, beauty has occurred 17 times in just a dozen pages; but then again, 'perfection' has already occurred 105 times, and 'culture', 152. More importantly, Arnold's 'beauty' has never been allowed to be simply beauty; every time it's been mentioned, it has always been accompanied by an ethical complement: '*divine* beauty', '*wisdom* and beauty', 'the beauty and *worth* of human nature', 'the idea of beauty and of a *human nature perfect on all its sides*' (twice), 'the idea of beauty, *harmony, and complete human perfection*' (also twice), plus seven slight variations on beauty and sweetness.

Beauty—moralized. *In Memoriam.* But there is more. 'Hitherto I have been insisting chiefly on beauty, or sweetness', Arnold goes on: beauty, that is to say sweetness. Sweetness? '. . . chiefly on beauty, or sweetness, as a character of perfection . . .' Beauty, or sweetness; sweetness, or perfection. Chinese boxes. Within boxes— 'in making sweetness and light to be characters of perfection, culture is of like spirit with poetry . . .'[81]—and boxes—'like religion— that other effort after perfection . . .'[82]—until we reach the Box of all Boxes: '. . . because, like religion—that other effort after perfection—it testifies that . . . he who works for sweetness and light, works to make reason and the will of God prevail'.[83]

Fog.

---

80 Matthew Arnold, *Culture and Anarchy*, Cambridge 2002 (1869), p. 81.
81 Ibid., p. 67.
82 Ibid., p. 78.
83 Ibid.

'Mistiness is the mother of wisdom', wrote Morley, sarcastically, in *On Compromise* (1874);[84] he probably wasn't thinking about Arnold, but he could have been: beauty, sweetness, light, perfection, poetry, religion, reason, the will of God . . . What is this? Are Arnold's concepts so new that they can only emerge by indirect approxima- tion? No; they aren't new at all; nor are they the type of notion—like 'child', 'heap', or 'red'—where a certain amount of vagueness is a condition of meaning.[85] Their porousness is, rather, a way of assert- ing the fundamental and immutable *unity* of culture. What is beautiful has to be *also* good *and* holy *and* true. The beginning of the Gothic revival, writes Kenneth Clark, was the decision to 'exclude technical terms' from the discussion on the new House of Parliament, and let 'simple human values take their place'.[86] Simple human values: men of culture, writes Arnold, 'have laboured to divest knowledge of all that was harsh, uncouth, difficult, abstract, professional, exclusive; to humanize it, to make it efficient outside the clique of the cultivated and learned'.[87] It's the 'ease, grace, and versatility' of the 'liberally educated' of Newman's *Idea of a University*;[88] Ruskin's crusade against 'mechanical' precision; or, again, Arnold's 'engaging conversational presence' as his 'most distinctive quality'.[89] And the result of all this . . .

The result is that culture must *not* be a profession. This is the source of the fog that pervades every page of *Culture and*

---

84   John Morley, *On Compromise*, Hesperides 2006, p. 39.
85   'Certain concepts are ineradicably vague', writes Michael Dummett, not in the sense 'that we could not sharpen them if we wished to; but, rather, that, by sharpening them, we should destroy their whole point.' Michael Dummett, 'Wang's Paradox', in Rosanna Keefe and Peter Smith, eds, *Vagueness: A Reader*, Cambridge, MA, 1966, p. 109.
86   Clark, *Gothic Revival*, p. 102.
87   Arnold, *Culture and Anarchy*, p. 79.
88   Newman, *Idea of a University*, p. 166.
89   Stefan Collini, 'Introduction' to *Culture and Anarchy*, Cambridge 2002, p. xi.

Anarchy: the ease and grace of the dilettante, drifting among great human values, without stooping to those mechanical definitions a professional would be bound to give. Not that Arnold's vagueness is therefore invincible: to know what he means by 'culture', for instance, we need only forget the vapid formulas for which he is famous—'the best that has been thought and known': fog—and look at the concordances of the term instead: and from within the opposition of culture and anarchy, a second one materializes, where culture gravitates around the idea of the State, and anarchy around the working class.[90] So, yes, one can dispel the fog, and decipher the message that was concealed underneath. But what if the fog were *itself* the message? Dror Wahrman:

> Between the poles of (radical) undivided inclusiveness and sharp (conservative) exclusiveness stood the 'middle class idiom'. The ability of its proponents to walk the fine line . . . was predicated on the fact that in terms of social signification *the language of 'middle class' was inherently vague*. Few of its proponents ever chose to define it or to specify its referents.[91]

---

90 'Culture suggests the idea of the State', writes Arnold near the end of the second section: 'we find no basis for a firm State-power in our ordinary selves; culture suggests one to us in our best self' (*Culture and Anarchy*, p. 99). And in the 'Conclusion': 'Thus, in our eyes, the very framework and exterior order of the State, whoever may administer the State, is sacred; and culture is the most resolute enemy of anarchy, because of the great hopes and designs for the State which culture teaches us to nourish' (p. 181). As for anarchy, in those cases where the term is linked to a recognizable social referent, it is with 'the Hyde Park rough' of working-class extraction (p. 89); in a particularly shameless moment, Arnold admits that 'doing what one likes' was 'convenient enough so long as there were only the Barbarians and the Philistines to do what they liked, but [is] getting inconvenient, and productive of anarchy, now that the Populace wants to do what it likes too' (p. 120).

91 Wahrman, *Imagining the Middle Class*, pp. 55–6.

Inherently vague. The category of middle class had 'an inherent vagueness in relation to social structures', he adds elsewhere, 'and indeed this vagueness often served the purpose of its users'.[92] Perfect, this elective affinity between the rhetoric of vagueness and the term that ousted 'bourgeois' from the English language. That semantic choice had been an act of symbolic camouflage, I wrote in the 'Introduction'; but then again, Victorianism is one long story of camouflage, from Gothic turrets to Christian gentlemen, from Tennyson's hypotaxis to Conrad's digressions, Carlyle's captains, and everybody's moralizing adjectives and eagerly promoted earnestness. Vagueness is what allows these spectres to survive the light of day; the fog that lays to rest the 'unmistakable definiteness' of prose, and with it the great intellectual wager of bourgeois literature.[93]

---

92   Ibid., pp. 8, 16.

93   In *Capitalism, Culture and Decline in Britain 1750–1990*, W. D. Rubinstein—whose earlier *Men of Property* remains a fundamental study of the Victorian upper class—makes exactly the opposite claim: 'In the course of the nineteenth century', he writes, 'educated English prose and discourse manifestly evolved in the direction of much greater clarity, cogency, and conciseness, to give it the elegance and precision which one now associates with the best English prose [and with] those precise, well-defined, and well-delineated modes we may associate with rationality and modernity' (*Capitalism, Culture and Decline in Britain 1750–1990*, London/New York 1993, p. 87). Rubinstein's two illustrative excerpts—from Orwell's 'Politics and the English Language', and, bizarrely, Nock's *Historic Railway Disasters*—are indeed clear and cogent. But are they also representative of two centuries of English prose? Orwell, for one, would have disagreed. The very essay Rubinstein quotes explicitly singles out 'the mixture of vagueness and sheer incompetence' as 'the most marked feature of modern English prose'. See 'Politics and the English Language' (1946), in George Orwell, *Collected Essays, Journalism, and Letters*, ed. Sonia Orwell and Ian Angus, Harmondsworth 1972, vol. IV, pp. 158–9.

4

'National Malformations':
Metamorphoses in the Semi-Periphery

I. BALZAC, MACHADO, AND MONEY

Shortly after his arrival in Paris, the hero of *Lost Illusions*, Lucien de Rubempré, gives the manuscript of his first novel to the book-seller Doguereau, in the hope that he may like it and publish it. Struck by the young writer's talent, Doguereau decides to offer him a thousand francs; on reaching Lucien's address, however, he changes his mind: 'A young man in such a lodging', he tells himself, 'has modest tastes . . . I need only pay him 800 francs.'[1] From the landlady, he learns that Lucien lives on the fourth floor, right under the roof: 600 francs. He knocks on the door, and a 'desperately bare' room appears, where all that can be seen are a bowl of milk and a piece of bread. 'This, Monsieur, is how Jean-Jacques lived', exclaims Doguereau; 'in such lodgings the flame of genius burns, and master-pieces are written'. And he offers 400 francs.

Half a century later, something quite similar occurs in Machado's *Posthumous Memoirs of Brás Cubas* (1881). During a journey from Coimbra to Lisbon, the donkey on which Brás is riding throws him from the saddle; his foot is caught in the stirrup, the donkey starts

---

1 Balzac, *Lost Illusions*, p. 205.

running, and things could end badly—'head split open, a conges-
tion, some kind of internal injury'—if it weren't for a muleteer who
manages to stop the donkey 'not without effort and danger'. On the
spur of the moment, Brás decides to give him three of the five gold
coins he has in his purse; while he's resting to regain his composure,
however, he begins to think 'that maybe the gratuity was excessive,
that two coins might be sufficient'. A few more moments, and 'As a
matter of fact, one coin was enough to make him quiver with joy.'
Eventually, Brás gives the muleteer a silver *cru*ᶎ*ado*; and as he rides
away, he still feels 'a little troubled'; he has 'paid him well, perhaps
too well. I put my fingers in the vest . . . and felt some copper
coins . . . which I should have given him instead of the silver
crusado.' After all, wasn't his presence a sign that he was 'an instrument of Providence', with no 'personal merit' in the act? This
thought, Brás concludes, 'made me miserable; I called myself waste-
ful . . . I felt (why not come right out with it?), I felt remorse.'[2]

Two episodes on how to pay as little as possible for someone's
labour. But their logic could not be more different. With
Doguereau—who is as close to 'capital personified' as literary characters get —personal feelings never enter the equation; he observes
the street, the building, the room, and proceeds to an objective
assessment of Lucien's market value: if someone lives on bread and
milk in a garret, his price drops. By contrast, there is nothing objective in Brás's succession of impulses, but only that 'subordination of
bourgeois reality to personal arbitrariness'[3] which Roberto Schwarz
has singled out as the centre of Machado's work: a 'victory of
caprice'[4] with 'no continuity of purpose whatsoever'.[5] Caprice;

2   *The Posthumous Memoirs of Brás Cubas*, Oxford 1997 (1881), pp. 47–8.
3   Roberto Schwarz, 'The Poor Old Woman and Her Portraitist', in
Misplaced Ideas, London 1992, p. 94.
4   Roberto Schwarz, *A Master on the Periphery of Capitalism*, Durham,
NC, 2001 (1990), p. 33.
5   Roberto Schwarz, 'Complex, Modern, National, and Negative', in

capricho; from the Italian *capra*, goat, with its unpredictable movements—and with the infantile connotations, too, that the term has never completely lost. With Machado's eternally immature heroes, small things become enormous, and important ones shrink to nothing: a character of *Quincas Borba* (1891) goes to a hanging on the spur of the moment, just to pass the time; while Bento, the protagonist of *Dom Casmurro* (1899) is annoyed by a friend who has spoilt his afternoon of daydreams by—dying. 'If Manduca could have waited a few hours to die, no discordant note would have come to interrupt the melodies of my soul. Why die exactly half an hour before? Any time is appropriate for dying.'[6]

Where nothing has its right measure any more, there flourishes the 'disproportional' (Sianne Ngai) feeling of *irritation*.[7] In Chapter 31 of *Brás Cubas*, a black butterfly enters Brás's room and alights on a painting, where 'the soft movement with which it began to move its wings . . . had a certain mocking way about it that bothered me a great deal'.[8] A few more minutes, and Brás feels a veritable 'nervous shock'; so he grabs a towel and strikes the butterfly. To kill it? Not really—though that's clearly likely to happen, if one hits a butterfly with a towel. But Brás doesn't think about consequences. And then, typically, the butterfly doesn't die, and Brás has time to 'regret' what he has done—Machado's characters are *always* feeling regret—and to indulge in a warm feeling of self-absolution. But no; the butterfly dies. And a second wave of irritation starts flowing, followed by a second absolution: 'I was a little upset, bothered: "Why the devil wasn't it blue?" I said to myself. And that reflection—one of the most profound that has been made since butterflies were invented—consoled me for my evil deed and reconciled me with myself.'[9]

Misplaced Ideas, p. 89.

6 J. M. Machado de Assis, *Dom Casmurro*, Oxford 1997, p. 152.
7 Sianne Ngai, *Ugly Feelings*, Cambridge, MA, 2005, p. 175.
8 J. M. Machado de Assis, *The Posthumous Memoirs of Brás Cubas*, p. 61.
9 Ibid., p. 62.

'The Black Butterfly' is 800 words long; the chapter with the muleteer, 900; Manduca's death, in *Dom Casmurro*, 700. It's the impact of
caprice on narrative tempo: 'no continuity of purpose', to repeat
Schwarz's words; the plot, disarticulated into a swarm of mini-
chapters—160 in *Brás Cubas*; 148 in *Dom Casmurro*; 201 in *Quincas
Borba*—where in a page or two a theme is evoked, developed, exag-
gerated, and dropped. At the end of the episode, caprice looks back
at what has just happened, and shrugs its shoulders: it could have
been otherwise. It *should* have been otherwise. Why wasn't it blue?
Why die half an hour before? It's a frontal attack on the bourgeois
reality principle, which reaches its apex in Bento's marvellous
version of double-entry bookkeeping: a perfectly accurate balance-
sheet where the creditor is—God:

> Ever since I was small I had become used to asking favors of heaven,
> promising prayers if they were granted. I said the first ones, the next
> were put off, and as they piled up they were gradually forgotten. In
> this way I got to twenty, thirty, fifty. I got into the hundreds, and
> now it was a thousand . . . I was loaded down with unfulfilled
> promises. The last had been two hundred paternosters and two
> hundred ave marias, if it didn't rain one afternoon on an outing to
> Santa Teresa. It didn't rain, but I didn't say the prayers.[10]

Loaded with unfulfilled promises. As her firstborn dies, Bento's
mother vows that—should her next son survive—he will become a
priest. The boy is born, and lives; now she must 'pay the debt'.[11] But
she no longer wants to. After many lucubrations, a family friend
finds the perfect solution: since she has 'promised God to give him
a priest', she *will* give him one; just not Bento. 'She can easily take
an orphan lad, and get him ordained', he explains; 'from the financial point of view, it was an easy matter . . . and an orphan would

---

10   Machado de Assis, *Dom Casmurro*, p. 41.
11   Ibid., p. 82.

not be in need of great luxuries . . .'[12] More sombrely—and grotesquely—Pérez Galdós's heartless usurer Torquemada, faced with his son's imminent death, grabs a roll of coins from his desk, and runs out into the night in a desperate search for beggars. Later, when his own death is approaching, he briskly asks the family chaplain: 'What must I do to be saved? Explain it quickly and with the plainness that has to be used in business.'[13] A long struggle between usurer and confessor ensues, with echoes of the deathbed scenes of medieval Christianity,[14] until Torquemada's last gasp— 'Conversion!'—leaves everybody in doubt: Was he thinking of his soul, or of the profits to be made from the national debt?

The precepts of religion, jumbled with the stratagems of money. We are moving towards the margins of the modern world-system, and this strange embrace between the old metaphysics and the new cash nexus is a sign of those 'national malformations' generated, to quote Schwarz one more time, by 'the grotesque and catastrophic march of capital'.[15] There will be differences of course, among stories emerging from Madrid and a small Sicilian town, from Poland or Russia; but the embattled coexistence of capitalism and the old regime, and the—at least temporary—triumph of the latter, are common to all, and create among them a strong family resemblance. This chapter is a chronicle of bourgeois defeats.

2. KEYWORDS VII: 'ROBA'

The protagonist of my next novel, writes Verga in the preface to *I Malavoglia* (1881), will be a 'tipo borghese': a new social category, in

---

12   Ibid., p. 171.
13   Benito Pérez Galdós, *Torquemada*, New York 1986 (1889–96), p. 534.
14   See Jacques LeGoff, *Your Money or Your Life: Economy and Religion in the Middle Ages*, New York 1990 (1986), passim.
15   Roberto Schwarz, 'Who Can Tell Me That This Character Is Not Brazil?', in *Misplaced Ideas*, p. 103.

the Sicily of the time. And indeed, as the hero of *Mastro-Don Gesualdo*
(1889) mixes for the first time with the town's old elite, at a party
early in the novel, he truly seems to belong to a new human species:
envious and malevolent, the local notables surround him, inquiring
with hypocritical concern about his first big loan; and he answers,
'tranquillamente'—'quietly', 'evenly'—'I didn't sleep a wink, those
nights.'[16] Didn't sleep: the emotion is strong. But so is Gesualdo's
lucidity. The others run around, prey to petty greed, furtive sexual
desires, or sheer physical hunger; Gesualdo remains 'serious, with
his chin in his hand, not saying a word'.[17] And the same happens a few
chapters later, at the yearly auction of the town's public lands: "'One
guinea fifteen! . . . One! . . . Two! . . ." "Two guineas!" replied don
Gesualdo, impassible.'[18] The notables scream, act out, threaten,
curse; Gesualdo remains seated, silent, polite, 'quietly continuing to
cast up his accounts in his pocketbook, that lay open on his knee.
Then he raised his head, and retorted in a calm voice . . .'[19]

A bourgeois in Sicily. In 'latecomer countries', writes Jürgen
Kocka, 'there is less continuity in the development from the pre-
industrial to the industrial period', and early entrepreneurs tend to
be *'homines novi* to a larger extent than in early-industrializing
countries'.[20] True: Gesualdo is a new man to an extent unimagina-

---

16   I have used D. H. Lawrence's 1923 translation of *Mastro-Don Gesualdo*
(Westport, 1976, p. 54), modifying it as little as possible.

17   Ibid., p. 63.

18   Ibid., p. 165.

19   Ibid. Verga kept working until the very last draft, to find the right tone
for his bourgeois hero. When asked about his future investments, for instance,
the Gesualdo of the penultimate version showed 'all his petulance of the peasant
sown in gold, and replied with a smirk that revealed his sharp shining teeth'
(*Mastro-Don Gesualdo*, 1888 version, Turin 1993, p. 503); a year later, in the
definitive text, all this has disappeared, and Gesualdo replies simply: 'We all do
what we can . . .'

20   Jürgen Kocka, 'Entrepreneurship in a Latecomer Country', in *Industrial
Culture and Bourgeois Society*, p. 71.

ble in English literature; where, say, Dickens's Bounderby claims to be one, but isn't, or Craik's Halifax, though poor, is 'the son of a gentleman'. But the trouble is, no new man can simply be 'new': the old world resists him, and distorts his plans in all sorts of ways, and in Gesualdo's case the pressure is inscribed in the book's very title: *Mastro-Don Gesualdo*. 'Mastro', as a small artisan—or even a manual labourer, as the mason Gesualdo initially is—would be called in nineteenth-century Sicily. But, mastro-*don*: the honorific ('sir', more or less) that was routinely used for the old ruling class. 'You should keep for the protagonist the title of mastro-don', writes Verga to his French translator, 'because it condenses the sarcastic nickname attached by public malevolence to the enriched worker.'[21] *Operaio arricchito*: Verga himself posits the worker as the substance of Gesualdo, and his wealth as a contingent predicate; and indeed, though Gesualdo raises himself well above the 'operaio' he initially was, that centaur-like nickname hangs over him until the very end. There are moments when things seem about to change,[22] but the shift from 'mastro' to 'don' is never definitive, and promptly revoked whenever Gesualdo's wealth is particularly resented, or, cruelly, when he is about to die. It's as if he never really left that initial party, where the town notables, who carefully use 'don Gesualdo' when they address him directly, revert contemptuously to 'mastro-don' as soon as he's out of earshot.[23]

---

21   Giovanni Verga, *Lettere al suo traduttore*, ed. F. Chiappelli, Firenze 1954, p. 139.

22   At the initial party, for instance, after a servant has announced him as 'mastro-don Gesualdo' the hostess immediately intervenes—'Animal! You say Don Gesualdo Motta, you fool!' (p. 36). The use of the first name, which was usual in addressing labourers, peasants, or servants, makes the transformation of 'mastro-don Gesualdo' into 'don Gesualdo Motta' even more significant.

23   The narrator, too, uses 'mastro-don' throughout the novel, though Verga's constant recourse to free indirect style makes the idea of a 'narrator'—as distinct from the voices of the characters in the story—rather questionable.

Mastro, and don: two *ancien régime* designations. And the bourgeois? Early in the novel, Gesualdo goes to check the work being
done on an oil-press; it is raining, and the workers are under a shel-
ter, playing pitch-penny. After a volley of insults—'Splendid! . . .
That's just what I like! . . . Enjoy yourselves! . . . Go on, your pay
runs just the same!'[24]—Gesualdo places himself among the others,
in the most dangerous position, under the mill-stone that needs to
be raised:

> Give me the bar! I'm not frightened! . . . While we stand cackling
> time is flying! But the pay remains the same, eh? . . . As if I had
> stolen the money I give you! . . . Heave! on that side! Don't bother
> about me, I've got a tough skin! Ready! . . . heave . . . ! Jesus with
> us! . . . Mary be praised! . . . a bit more! . . . Ah, Mariano! Saints
> and devils you're killing me! Heave! . . . Mary be praised! . . . For
> your life! for your life! . . . Heave! . . . What are you doing, fool,
> over there? . . . Heave! . . . it's coming! . . . We've done it! . . .
> again! . . . on that side! . . . Don't be afraid that the Pope's going to
> die! . . . Want . . . now then! now! . . . want brings the wolf . . .
> again! . . . heave! . . . the wolf out of the wood![25]

In this amazing texture of breathless cries, the Gesualdo who speaks
as one of the workers (it's coming! . . . We've done it!), or appeals
to a shared religious (Jesus with us! . . . Mary be praised!) or prover-
bial (want brings the wolf out of the wood!) substratum, takes turns
with the undisputable, abusive master (Mariano! Saints and devils
you're killing me! . . . What are you doing, fool?). The *tertium* of
the 'tipo borghese'—serious, silent, impassible, calm—has decom-
posed into the two older categories; his quiet abstraction, shattered
by irrational impulses. 'You've got so much money, yet you throw

---

24   Verga, *Mastro-Don Gesualdo*, p. 69.
25   Ibid., p. 71.

your soul to the devil!'[26] cries his associate, the canon-priest Lupi, and he is right; there is something inexplicable in Gesualdo risking his life under the mill-stone (and then again, later, in the river that has just swept his bridge away). But he is not alone in this; another worker-entrepreneur from the semi-periphery, Gorky's Ilya Artamanov, having just celebrated a festival with his workers, notices a big boiler that has remained stuck in the sand, and, like Gesualdo, proceeds to lift it with his own hands; less fortunate than Gesualdo, he bursts a blood vessel and dies.[27] And one wonders: Why these scenes of almost mythical brutality, with their Sisyphean struggle against the force of gravity? Not even Robinson, alone on his island, does anything of the sort. Why does Gesualdo risk his life like that?

He does it, because he is terrified that his wealth may disappear: a fear that is always with him, even in the only peaceful moment of the entire novel, the so-called 'idyll' of the Canziria. In this little estate at some distance from town, Gesualdo 'felt his heart expand. Many pleasant memories came back to him.'[28] Pleasant? That's not what the novel says. 'How many stones had he carried on his back, before he built that store-barn!' the narrative goes on; how many 'days without bread':

> Always on the go, always tired, always on his feet, here, there, in sun, and wind, and rain; his head heavy with thoughts, his heart big with anxiety, his bones broken with weariness; snatching a couple of hours of sleep when he could, where he could, in a corner of the stable, behind a hedge, in the yard, with stones under his back; eating a piece of hard black bread wherever he was, on the mule's

---

26 Ibid., p. 74.
27 Maxim Gorky, *Decadence*, Lincoln, NE, 1984 (*The Artamanov's Business*, 1925), p. 80.
28 Verga, *Mastro-Don Gesualdo*, p. 85.

pack-saddle, in the shadow of an olive-tree, on the side of a ditch, in the malaria, amid a swarm of mosquitoes.—No holidays, no Sundays, never a merry laugh, everybody wanting something from him, his time, his work, or his money . . . In the village, not one who wasn't his enemy, or his dangerous and feared ally.—Always having to hide the fever of money-making, or the blow of a piece of bad news, or the rush of satisfaction; always keeping his face shut, his eye vigilant, his mouth serious![29]

Tired, on his feet, wind, rain, heavy, broken, anxiety, weariness, fear, hard bread, malaria, mosquitoes, enemies . . . And why? For *la roba*. 'Property', is Lawrence's usual translation, and in English one can't do much better.[30] But *roba*—a word that haunts Verga's novel, where it occurs over a hundred times—possesses an emotional significance that 'property' will never have. 'Who would be there to defend his property after his death?' muses Gesualdo, as he approaches the end: 'alas, poor property!'[31] Alas poor property? It sounds almost grotesque; but *povera roba* doesn't, because *roba* is not an abstract term; it means land, buildings, animals, fields, trees; among the poor, the objects of everyday life. *Roba* can be seen, touched, smelled; it's physical, often alive. It is an old notion, which unites the new man and the proud noblewoman Rubiera;[32] but *roba* is even older than Sicilian latifundia; its etymon is the Germanic *Raub*: booty, prey, loot (from which also the Italian *rubare*, 'stealing'). Thinking of the *Raubtiere*—the blond 'beasts of prey' of

29   Ibid., pp. 87–8.
30   Property is also the default option in the more recent translation by Giovanni Cecchetti (Berkeley, CA, 1979).
31   Verga, *Mastro-Don Gesualdo*, p. 436.
32   On the topic of *roba*, Rubiera and Gesualdo are virtually interchangeable: his 'I have killed myself with work . . . I have killed myself getting the *roba* together . . .' (p. 188) returns in her '[my ancestors] didn't kill themselves with work so that their *roba* should fall into the hands of just anybody' (p. 32). And the verbal parallelisms could be easily multiplied.

Nietsche's *Genealogy*—is probably too much for the word; but a trace of that 'capital dripping with blood and dirt' of Marx's 'primitive accumulation' is certainly present there. A predatory vitality trails *roba* through the novel, from Rubiera's being 'stuck like an oyster to her *roba*'[33] to Gesualdo 'passing his tongue over his lips as if he already tasted the sweet of the good morsel, like the man greedy of *roba* which he was'.[34] This is more than the 'fusion of person and thing' evoked by Auerbach for Balzac's great descriptions; *roba* is not a second skin, like Madame Vacquer's clothes; it is the 'blood' that Gesualdo sees 'squandered in the water' with the collapse of his bridge. *Roba* is life; it's that surplus of energy that was needed, in one form or another, for the take-off of capitalism in a peripheral country. *Roba* is life; hence also, fatally, death: that's where the irrational, overwhelming fear of losing it comes from. 'Assassin!' cries Rubiera, paralyzed in her bed, to her dissolute son: 'No! I won't let him devour my *roba*!' The dying Gesualdo wants 'his *roba* to go with him, desperate as he was',[35] *disperata come lui.* And Mazzarò, the protagonist of the short story 'La roba', when he's told that 'it was time to leave his *roba*, and to think about his soul', walks into the courtyard with a stick, staggering, like a madman, 'and he went around killing his ducks and his turkeys and crying, "*Roba mia, roba mia*, come away with me!"'

Roba is not abstract property; nor is Gesualdo that 'capital personified' that made an interesting bourgeois hero so hard to imagine. They are both concrete, alive; that's why they are so memorable— and vulnerable. As Gesualdo dies, and his *roba* is pocketed by his 'gentilissimo' son-in-law, the Duke of Leyra, the waters of the old regime seem to close forever over Verga's *tipo borghese.*

---

33 Verga, *Mastro-Don Gesualdo*, p. 279.
34 Ibid., p. 282.
35 Ibid., pp. 429–30.

3. Persistence of the Old Regime I: *The Doll*

The protagonist of Prus's *The Doll* (1890), Stanisław Wokulski, is introduced to the reader, in the novel's opening chapter, by a group of anonymous Warsaw restaurant-goers—similar, in their function as unreliable chorus, to the notables of Verga's party—who wonder aloud about the unprecedented novelty of this man who, 'though he had an assured living', had left Poland with all his money 'to make a fortune in the war': 'it was millions, he wanted'.[36] And millions he makes, 'amidst bullets, knives and typhus',[37] as he relates to Ignacy Rzecki, the timorous clerk and occasional narrator of *The Doll*. But Wokulski is more than just a capitalist adventurer; as a young man, while working as a waiter, he makes his way into college, where he studies Polish and European literatures; later he goes to Paris, where he develops a keen interest in modern technology. Bourgeois of property *and* bourgeois of culture; and again, not just that: in 1863, Wokulski takes part in the insurrection against the Russian occupation of Poland, and is deported to Siberia. All in all, he may be the most complete bourgeois figure of nineteenth-century fiction: financially sharp, intellectually curious, and politically daring. But with one fatal flaw: his infatuation for the young countess Isabella Lecki. 'Something not unlike a superstition was beginning to take shape in his realistic mind',[38] comments the narrator, as Wokulski starts taking all sorts of random events as omens of Isabella's feelings towards him; 'there are two men in me', reflects Wokulski himself: 'one quite sensible, and the other a lunatic'.[39] And, as *The Doll* unfolds, the lunatic wins.

He wins, because lunacy is endemic in the European semi-periphery at the turn of the century: from Mazzarò's slaughter of his

---

36   Boleslaw Prus, *The Doll*, New York 1972 (1890), pp. 1–4.
37   Ibid., p. 29.
38   Ibid., p. 195.
39   Ibid., p. 235.

animals in 'La roba', to the 'buying craze' of Rosalía Bringas in Galdós's *La de Bringas* (1884), or Guillermina Pacheco's 'militant charity' in *Fortunata y Jacinta* (1887). Torquemada twice loses his mind, at the beginning and at the end of his saga; Machado's Quincas Borba leaves a will requiring that his dog be treated 'like a human being'; Matilde Serao's Neapolitan fresco, *Il paese di cuccagna* (1890), is a kaleidoscope of superstition revolving around the lottery; while Dostoevsky's unbalanced characters are too many to be even mentioned. Lunacy is endemic, in the semi-periphery, because in these societies caught in the middle, where economic waves originating in the capitalist core strike with unfathomable and hyperbolic violence, irrational conduct becomes a sort of reflex, which reproduces the course of the world at the scale of individual existence. But even so, Wokulski's case is unique. 'A businessman in love!' writes Fredric Jameson, concentrating his incredulity in the exclamation mark;[40] and in love with someone who is no more than a spoiled child. 'She had become a mystic point where all his memories, longings and hopes coincided, a hearth without which his life would have neither sense nor meaning',[41] reflects Wokulski in the important chapter entitled 'Meditations'; and readers of *The Doll* look at these words in disbelief. Isabella, a mystic point? This *is* madness.

Once again, the European context suggests an answer. In the years of *The Doll*, writes Kocka, 'the upper stratum of the middle class came very close to the aristocracy [via] intermarriage and other forms of mixing'.[42] Marrying into old aristocratic families is precisely what Gesualdo and Torquemada do—and theirs are two excellent business deals, both mediated by a third character (Lupi in

---

40 Fredric Jameson, 'A Businessman in Love', in Franco Moretti, ed., *The Novel*, vol. II: *Forms and Themes*, Princeton, NJ, 2006.

41 Prus, *The Doll*, p. 75.

42 Kocka, *Industrial Culture and Bourgeois Society*, p. 247.

Gesualdo, and Donoso in *Torquemada*), as if to emphasize the fundamentally 'social' nature of their matrimonial choice. But if Verga
and Galdós use hypergamy to show the (seeming) permeability of
the old elite to bourgeois wealth, in Prus the episode emphasizes by
contrast the rigidity of the barriers between classes. Had he 'made a
fortune for himself and fallen in love with an aristocratic young
lady' in Paris, Wokulski reflects, 'he would not have encountered
so many obstacles';[43] but in Warsaw, though he is close enough to
western Europe to *imagine* his aristocratic romance, he is too far to
actually *realize* it. He is like a mutation rejected by his own ecosystem; a strange creature that ends up 'squandering his powers and his
life' in an impossible struggle '"with an environment into which I
didn't fit." . . . And at this moment, for the first time, the idea of not
returning to Poland appeared clearly to him.'[44]

Not returning to Poland. 'By bringing from distant lands our
forms of life, our institutions, and our vision of the world',
writes Sérgio Buarque about another peripheral modernity, 'we
were exiles in our own land'.[45] 'Everything I know . . . does not
come from here', echoes Wokulski.[46] He 'only breathed freely
when he reached Siberia', we read early in the book:[47] in actual
exile. When he returns to Poland, he immediately leaves again
for the war. Back from that, he is soon off to Paris; and then,
after another brief period in Warsaw, he disappears altogether
(rumour has him in Moscow, Odessa, India, China, Japan,
America . . .) Exile in his own land. He returns one last time, in
secret, to blow himself up under Isabella's country mansion.

---

43   Ibid., p. 385.
44   Ibid., p. 386.
45   Buarque's *Raízes do Brasil* is quoted by Roberto Schwarz in 'Misplaced
Ideas: Literature and Society in Late Nineteenth-Century Brazil' (1973), now in
his *Misplaced Ideas*, p. 20.
46   Prus, *The Doll*, p. 411.
47   Ibid., p. 74.

'He died under the ruins of feudalism', a friend laconically comments.[48]

The bourgeois as exile. And in fact, when Wokulski decides to sell his business 'lock, stock, and barrel', it is to the archetypal exiles: the Jews; the only ones 'as despised and ill-used as you are',[49] as his friend Szuman, who is himself a Jew, puts it. And Wokulski knows it: 'There was no one else in the whole country able to develop his ideas; no one, except the Jews'.[50] In part, given the financial role of Jews in eastern Europe, the episode is a sign of historical accuracy on Prus's part.[51] But there is more. No one except the Jews, yes; but then the quote continues: '. . . except the Jews—who had come forward with all their arrogance of race, their cunning, their ruthlessness . . .'[52] : 'In view of this', Wokulski concludes, 'he felt such a horror for commerce, trading companies and profits of any kind that he was surprised by himself.' Commerce, trading and profits have been Wokulski's life; but they now turn into horror, because Szlangbaum and the other Jews—just like the Quaker mill-owner Fletcher in *Halifax*, or the other first-generation industrialists of the English novel—show them for what they are, undiluted; because, in other words, they reveal *the truth of the bourgeois*. Or more precisely: the truth, *according to Isabella Lecki*. In a definitive act of submission to the old regime, Wokulski sees Szlangbaum exactly as Isabella sees him. His anti-Semitism, is the bourgeois turning against himself.

---

48   Ibid., p. 696.
49   Ibid., p. 629.
50   Ibid., p. 635.
51   Towards the end of the century, writes Kocka, 'in Poland, the Czech and Slovak areas, Hungary and Russia, the owners of capital, entrepreneurs and managers were often foreign nationals: frequently Germans and unassimilated Jews'. Jürgen Kocka, 'The European Pattern and the German Case', in Kocka and Mitchell, eds, *Bourgeois Society in Nineteenth-Century Europe*, p. 21.
52   Prus, *The Doll*, p. 635.

I began this section with a portrait of Wokulski as a great bourgeois figure; I am ending it with another study in self-contradiction, as destructive as Verga's impossible conjunction of *mastro* and *don*. The old world brings discord into the lives of these new men, and cruelty to their deaths: held prisoner in a ducal palace by jeering underlings, Gesualdo; buried 'under the ruins of feudalism', Wokulski. In the next section, we will encounter one more variation on the same theme.

4. Persistence of the Old Regime II: *Torquemada*

In Pérez Galdós's crowded frescoes of nineteenth-century Spain, the *Torquemada* tetralogy (1889–96) stands out for its unswerving focus on its central character, the usurer and slum-landlord Torquemada, whom we follow from the 'murky transactions' of plebeian Madrid to the financial triumphs and aristocratic alliances that bring him to be 'hand in glove with the State itself'. But his rise coincides with a growing sense of self-estrangement: having promised his dying friend Doña Lupe (another usurer) to marry one of the Aguila sisters, from an impoverished aristocratic family, Torquemada ends up being ruled by his sister-in-law Cruz, who eventually strong-arms him into acquiring a marquisate, complete with a palace and painting-gallery. Persistence of the Old Regime: an energetic self-made man who 'draws closer to the old ruling classes, instead of contesting their primacy'.[53] Nor is this 'drawing closer' the stylish symbiosis of James, Schnitzler, or Proust; just as the cracks on Gesualdo's hands reveal the mason under the 'don', an ancient plebeian hunger urges Torquemada to devour—a few hours before his wedding—a plate of raw onions that 'went very badly with the fine words' of the aristocratic event.[54] And at the end of the book another meal—his last attempt to return to his roots:

---

53 Mayer, *The Persistence of the Old Regime*, p. 208.
54 Pérez Galdós, *Torquemada*, p. 352.

'give me a plate of stewed beans, by gum, for it's time for a fellow to be of the people, and go back to the people, to nature, so to speak!'[55]—leads to a monumental diarrhoea, and an interminable agony.

But Torquemada is far from being only a coarse physical presence. 'You are *exaggeration personified*', he tells Cruz, as she opens her campaign for the marquisate; 'and since I *make a boast of* the fact that I'm the golden mean *personified*, I put everything in its proper place, and refute your arguments as of the present historical moment.'[56] It's his language, more than his body, that makes Torquemada unforgettable. Which is strange, because, usually, characters who are involved in shady business deals—Gobseck, Merdle, Bulstrode, Werle . . . —tend to be taciturn to the point of secretiveness. Torquemada, not in the least:

> 'I wash my hands: I *make a boast* of obeying the man who rules and of not *infringing the laws*. I respect *Greeks and Trojans alike*, and do not haggle over the *obol* of tribute. *By dint* of being a practical man, I don't engage in systematic opposition, nor do I engage in *Machiavellianisms* of any kind whatever. I am *refractory* to intrigue . . .'[57]

Flat-footed attempts at classical erudition ('Greeks and Trojans', 'Machiavellianisms'); dead metaphors ('I wash my hands', 'I make a boast'); ponderous truisms ('the present historical moment'). Money has given Don Francisco a chance to make himself heard in society; he now speaks 'in a louder voice',[58] and, like his progenitor Monsieur Jourdain, he wants to 'raisonner des choses parmi les

---

55 Ibid., p. 515.
56 Ibid., p. 226. The emphases throughout this section are all in the original.
57 Ibid., p. 385.
58 Ibid., p. 9.

honnêtes gens'. And so, inevitably, he becomes a target for ridicule; this weapon 'often deployed in the conflict among classes . . . and extremely effective in keeping . . . the rich bourgeois in their place'.[59] In Torquemada's case, ridicule concentrates on a very specific linguistic tic:

> 'My intention, mind you! was to give you an indication . . . I am a considerate man and know how to make distinctions. Believe me, I had quite a bad moment when I became aware, after leaving, of my slip, of my . . . *stupefaction.*'

> Don Francisco replied in stumbling, hurried sentences, without saying anything specific, merely that he *cherished the conviction* that . . . and that he had made those *manifestations* to Señor Donoso moved by pity . . . no, moved by the noblest sentiment (by this time we were all too noble for words); that his desire to be acceptable to the Aguila ladies *exceeded all ponderation* . . .

> 'I must manifest a few badly expressed . . . manifestations which, though poor in style and crude as literature, will be the *sincere* expression of a grateful heart . . . Let's pay more attention to action than to words; let's work, work a lot and speak little. Work always, *in accordance* with our needs and with *the valuable accompaniment* of all the elements that *accompany* us. And, having made these manifestations, which I believe were called upon me by my presence in this august place . . . having made these declarations . . .'[60]

Intention, indication, distinction, stupefaction, opposition, conviction, manifestation, ponderation, expression, declaration . . . Like a

---

59   Francesco Fiorentino, *Il ridicolo nel teatro di Molière*, Turin 1997, pp. 67, 80–1.

60   Pérez Galdós, *Torquemada*, pp. 96, 131–2, 380, 383–4.

moth near a candle, Torquemada is hypnotized by *nominaliza-tions*: that class of words that take the 'actions and processes' commonly expressed by verbs, and turn them into nouns that indicate 'abstract objects [and] generalized processes'.[61] Because of this semantic peculiarity, nominalizations are frequent in scientific prose—where abstract objects and generalized processes are usually important—and *in*-frequent, by contrast, in oral exchanges, which tend to focus on what is concrete and unique. But if this is so, why then does Torquemada use them every time he opens his mouth?

'What exactly', wonders Erich Auerbach, 'was a bourgeois in seventeenth-century France?' In terms of his social position he could of course be a variety of things—a doctor, a merchant, a lawyer, a shop-keeper, an officer, and more. But whatever he was, the highest symbolic value of the age—*honnêteté*: an 'ideal of universality . . . to which the upper bourgeoisie had come to aspire'—forced him to 'gloss over' his economic existence, because only 'a man cleansed of all particular qualities' would be considered worthy of it.[62] Two hundred years later, Torquemada's nominalizations respond to a comparable social imperative: they are an attempt at erasing from his language the old 'paymaster of hell',[63] by trying to elevate everything to a plane of disembodied abstraction. Trying, and of course failing. It's the 'deterioration of protagonicity' that Fredric Jameson has recently noticed in the *Torquemada* cycle: the same man who—despite being 'technically a minor character'—had been the secret protagonist of other Galdós novels, turns suddenly into 'a flat minor character' in the books

---

61   Douglas Biber, Susan Conrad and Randi Reppen, *Corpus Linguistics: Investigating Language Structure and Use*, Cambridge 1998, pp. 61ff.
62   Erich Auerbach, 'La cour et la ville' (1951), in *Scenes from the Drama of European Literature*, Minneapolis, MN, 1984, pp. 152, 172, 168, 165.
63   Pérez Galdós, *Torquemada*, p. 3.

where he is nominally the protagonist.[64] It's a strange reversal, it's true, and, as for other formal paradoxes we have already encountered, Torquemada's 'deterioration' is not just a matter of form, but a consequence of *the objective dialectic of the usurer in modern society*: full of energy and insight as long as he can live in the shade, as the parasitical and sinister double—'technically a minor character'—of modern banking, the paymaster of hell turns into a disoriented windbag if he is forced to show his face in public. This was your secret hero, Galdós seems to be saying to the Spanish bourgeoisie—and this is his vacuity, when he tries to speak the language of universality. In Torquemada's 'ponderations' and 'stupefactions', the hegemonic ambitions of a whole class are buried in ridicule.

5. 'There's arithmetic for you!'

If one were to look for a flawless bourgeois nature, the young manager Stolz—German for 'pride'—who appears in one of the great Russian novels of the nineteenth century, would be an excellent choice. Though 'constantly in motion', the perfectly efficient Stolz never makes 'an unnecessary movement', and when his childhood friend, bewildered by his activity, interrupts him with a meek 'One day, you too will stop working . . .' he replies, simply: 'Never. Why should I?' (And then adds, with words worthy of Faust: 'Oh, if only I could live two hundred years, or three . . . imagine all I could accomplish . . .') German on his father's side—so that his aristocratic Russian mother fears he will 'turn into a *Bürger*'—Stolz is a living link with the dynamism of western Europe, with which his company is constantly trading. Halfway through the novel, he travels to Paris, and makes his friend promise that he will soon join him there, to start a new existence together. It's a good life, for a bourgeois in eastern Europe: Stolz is active, serene, intelligent; he buys a beautiful estate, marries the woman he loves, is happy . . .

---

64   Fredric Jameson, *The Antinomies of Realism* (forthcoming from Verso).

He receives everything he could wish for, from the author of his novel, except for the most important thing: he is not the protagonist of *Oblomov*.[65]

He is not the protagonist, because Goncharov is fascinated by his colossal, wonderful Oblomov. Still, that Stolz's textbook bourgeois nature should be so clearly *not* what the novel is about is the sign of a larger problem. Not that Russian literature is indifferent to the new power of money; in the Petersburg of *Crime and Punishment*, having money is (at least) as decisive as in Dickens's London, or in Zola's Paris. But it is so in a very specific way: from the greed of the old pawnbroker Alyona Ivanovna to the student's pitiless tirade on her murder, to Marmeladov's drunken beggary, Sonja's wordless prostitution, its echo in Dunya's engagement ('she'll sell herself for those who are dear to her'), all the way to the 'university lecturer in world history' who forges lottery tickets[66]—through all these, and more, all that money can do is generate hyperbolic distortions of modern economic behaviour. In the West, money tends to simplify things; here, it complicates them. There is too little of it around— and too expensive. In lieu of western Europe's low and stable interest rates, what echoes through Dostoevsky's pages is Alyona's whisper to Raskolnikov: 'ten percent a month, dearie. Payable in advance.'[67]

Ten per cent a month. Under such unbearable pressure, 'national malformations' become inevitable. Take utilitarianism. In 1825, the anonymous author of an article in the *Westminster Review* declared, 'in sober and utilitarian sadness', that he would be 'extremely glad to be informed, how the universal pursuit of literature and poetry,

---

65   Ivan Goncharov, *Oblomov*, New York 2008 (1859), pp. 167, 174–5, 198, 345, 432.
66   Fyodor Dostoevsky, *Crime and Punishment*, Harmondsworth 1991 (1866), pp. 102, 76, 49, 43–60, 196.
67   Ibid., p. 39.

poetry and literature, is to conduce towards cotton-spinning'.[68] It's a philistine ultimatum that finds an almost literal echo, a generation later, in Turgenev's *Fathers and Sons* (1862), when Bazarov offhand-edly declares, with his characteristic insolence, that 'a decent chemist is twenty times more useful than any poet'.[69] Useful. But for Bazarov this is no longer the concrete, pragmatic keyword of *Robinson* and the Victorians: it is a force for change—for destruc-tion, even. 'We act on the basis of what we recognize as useful', he adds in a later scene, to explain the logic of nihilism: 'nowadays the most useful thing of all is rejection—and we reject.'[70]

Utility as the foundation of nihilism. The *Westminster Review* would have been stunned. And Bazarov was just the beginning:

Look: on the one hand you have a nasty, stupid, worthless, mean-ingless, sick old woman who's no use to anyone and is, indeed, actually harmful to people . . . on the other hand you have young, fresh energies that are going to waste for lack of backing—thou-sands of people are involved, and it's happening everywhere! . . . Instead of one life, thousands of lives rescued from corruption and decay. One death to a hundred lives—I mean, there's arithmetic for you![71]

There's arithmetic! Bentham's 'felicific calculus', leading to murder. 'If you take your ideas to their ultimate conclusions', Raskolnikov comments, after the obtuse Westernizer Luzhin has delivered his paean to progress—'more, as it were, criticism; more effi-ciency . . .'—then 'the end result would be that it's all right to go

68   'Present System of Education', *Westminster Review*, July–October 1825, p. 166.
69   Ivan Turgenev, *Fathers and Sons*, New York 2008 (1862), p. 20.
70   Ibid., p. 38.
71   Dostoevsky, *Crime and Punishment*, pp. 101–2.

around killing people'.[72] From criticism and efficiency, to going around killing people. Misplaced ideas: in Dostoevsky's Russia, Schwarz's great metaphor for the misfit between Western models and Brazilian reality works perhaps even better than in the original. In Machado, the discord between the two had remained largely harmless: plenty of voluble irresponsibility, but few major consequences. But in Russia, a radical, proletarianized intelligentsia takes Western ideas *too seriously*, pushing them truly 'to their ultimate conclusions' indeed:

> Roman Jakobson claims that the Russian word for the everyday— *byt*—is culturally untranslatable into Western languages; according to Jakobson, only Russians among the European nations are capable of fighting 'the fortresses of byt' and of conceptualizing a radical alterity to the everyday.[73]

The everyday. For Auerbach, it was the solid, unquestionable foundation of nineteenth-century realism. Here, it's a fortress to be stormed. 'Dostoevsky loved the word "suddenly" [*vdrug*]', writes Viktor Shklovsky; 'a word about the fractured nature of life, the unevenness of its steps'.[74] Dostoevsky's poetics requires 'the creation of extraordinary situations for the provoking and testing of a philosophical idea', adds Bakhtin: 'points of crisis, turning points and catastrophes [when] everything is unexpected, out of place, incompatible and impermissible if judged by life's ordinary, "normal" course'.[75] It's the hatred for compromise so typical of

---

72   Ibid., pp. 192–7.
73   Svetlana Boym, *Common Places: Mythologies of Everyday Life in Russia*, Cambridge, MA, 1994, p. 3.
74   Viktor Shklovsky, *Energy of Delusion: A Book on Plot*, Champaign, IL, 2007 (1981), p. 339.
75   Mikhail Bakhtin, *Problems of Dostoevsky's Poetics*, Minneapolis, MN, 1984 (1929–63), pp. 114, 149, 146.

Dostoevsky's characters;[76] the absence of a 'neutral' zone in Russian culture, discovered by Lotman and Uspenskij in their study of dualistic cultural models;[77] the extreme oscillations described in the pages on the Russian novel in *Mimesis*.[78] It's the most radical of all the 'national malformations' we have seen in these pages: an uncanny radicalization of Western ideas that liberates their destructive potential. It's Bazarov's German science that makes his nihilism so breathtakingly unforgiving; it's English arithmetic that generates the most enigmatically significant crime of modern literature. It's like an extreme experiment being run in front of our eyes: placing bourgeois values *as far as possible from their original context*, to capture their unique mix of greatness and catastrophe. In the years immediately following, Ibsen's 'realistic' cycle performed exactly the opposite experiment—and reached the same conclusions.

---

76   'I would thou wert cold or hot', recites the holy fool Tikhon in *Devils*, quoting from John's *Apocalypse*: 'So then, because thou art lukewarm, and neither cold nor hot, I will spue thee out of my mouth.' Fyodor Dostoevsky, *Devils*, Oxford 1992 (1871), p. 458.

77   'In the Catholic Christian West', they write, 'life after death is divided into three zones: paradise, purgatory and hell. Similarly life on earth is thought of as demonstrating three types of behavior: definitely sinful, definitely holy, and a neutral kind . . . a wide band of neutral behavior and . . . neutral social institutions . . . This neutral sphere becomes a structural reserve from which tomorrow's system develops.' But Russian Christianity, Lotman and Uspenskij go on, emphasized by contrast a 'marked dualism' that left no room 'for an intermediate zone'; so that, inevitably 'behavior in this life becomes either sinful or holy'. Jurij M. Lotman and Boris A. Uspenskij, 'The Role of Dual Models in the Dynamics of Russian Culture (Up to the End of the Eighteenth Century)', in Ann Shukman, ed., *The Semiotics of Russian Culture*, Ann Arbor, MI, 1984, p. 4.

78   'A strong practical, ethical, or intellectual shock immediately arouses them in the depths of their instincts, and in a moment they pass from a quiet and almost vegetative existence to the most monstrous excesses both in practical and in spiritual matters. The pendulum of their vitality, of their actions, thoughts, and emotions, seems to oscillate farther than elsewhere in Europe' (Auerbach, *Mimesis*, p. 523).

5

Ibsen and the Spirit of Capitalism

I. THE GREY AREA

First of all, the social universe of Ibsen's cycle: shipbuilders, industrialists, financiers, merchants, bankers, developers, administrators, judges, managers, lawyers, doctors, headmasters, professors, engineers, pastors, journalists, photographers, designers, accountants, clerks, printers . . . No other writer has focused so single-mindedly on the bourgeois world. Mann; but in Mann there is a constant dialectic of bourgeois and artist (Thomas and Hanno, Lübeck and Kröger, Zeitblom and Leverkühn), and in Ibsen not quite; his one great artist—the sculptor Rubek, in *When We Dead Awaken* (1899), who will 'work until the day he dies', and loves to be 'lord and master over his material'—is a bourgeois exactly like all the others.[1]

Social historians sometimes have doubts on whether a banker and a photographer, or a shipbuilder and a pastor, are really part of the same class. In Ibsen, they are; or at least, they share the same spaces, and speak the same language. None of the English 'middle' class camouflage, here; this is not a class in the middle,

---

1   Henrik Ibsen, *The Complete Major Prose Plays*, translated and introduced by Rolf Fjelde, New York 1978, pp. 1064, 1044. Many thanks to Sarah Allison for her help with the Norwegian original.

overshadowed from those above it, and innocent of the course of the world; this is the *ruling* class, and the world is what it is because they have *made* it that way. This is why Ibsen is the epilogue of this book: his plays are the great 'settling of accounts' of the bourgeois century, to use one of his metaphors. He is the only writer who looks the bourgeois in the face, and asks: So, finally, what have you brought into the world?

I will return to this question, of course. For now, let me just say how strange it is to have such a broad bourgeois fresco—and no workers in it, except for a few house servants. *Pillars of Society* (1877), which is the first play of the cycle, is different in this respect; it opens with a confrontation between a union leader and a dockyard manager on the importance of safety versus that of profits; and although the theme is never at the centre of the plot, it is visible throughout, and is decisive in shaping its ending. But after *Pillars*, the conflict between capital and labour disappears from Ibsen's world, even though, in general, *nothing* disappears here: *Ghosts* (1881) is such a perfect Ibsen title because so many of his characters *are* ghosts: the minor figure of one play returns as the protagonist in another, or the other way around; a wife leaves her home at the end of one play, and stays to the bitter end in the following one . . . It's like a twenty-year-long experiment Ibsen is running: changing a variable here and there, to see what happens to the system. But no workers in the experiment—even though these are the years when trade unions, socialist parties, and anarchism are changing the face of European politics.

No workers, because the conflict Ibsen wants to focus on is *internal* to the bourgeoisie itself. Four works make this particularly clear: *Pillars of Society*; *The Wild Duck* (1884); *Masterbuilder Solness* (1892); *John Gabriel Borkman* (1896). Four plays with the same prehistory, in which two business partners, and/or friends, have engaged in a desperate struggle, in the course of which one of them has been financially ruined, and psychically maimed. Intra-bourgeois competition is a mortal combat, here, and it becomes easily ruthless; but, and this is important, ruthless, unfair, equivocal, murky—yet seldom actually *illegal*. In a few cases it's also that, as with the forgeries of *Dollhouse* (1879), or the water pollution in *An Enemy of the People* (1882), or some of Borkman's financial manoeuvres. But, typically, Ibsen's wrongdoings occur in an elusive grey area whose nature is never completely clear.

This grey area is Ibsen's great intuition about bourgeois life, so let me give a few examples of what it looks like. In *Pillars of Society* there are rumours that a theft has occurred in Bernick's firm; he knows that the rumours are false, but he is also aware that they will save him from bankruptcy; and so, though they destroy a friend's reputation, he lets them circulate; later, he uses political influence in a barely legal way, to protect investments that are themselves barely legal. In *Ghosts*, pastor Manders persuades Mrs Alving not to insure her orphanage, so that public opinion won't think that 'neither you nor I have adequate faith in Divine Providence';[2] divine providence being what it is, the orphanage burns down—probably, though not certainly, because of arson—and all is lost. There is the 'trap' that Werle might (or might not) have laid for his partner in the prehistory of *The Wild Duck*, and the unclear business between Solness and *his* partner in the prehistory of *The Masterbuilder*; where there is also a chimney that should be repaired, and isn't, and the house burns down—but, the insurance experts say, for a wholly different reason . . .

This is what the grey area is like: reticence, disloyalty, slander, negligence, half truths . . . As far as I can tell, there is no general term for these actions; which at first, given my reliance on keywords as clues to bourgeois values, I found quite frustrating.

---

2   Ibid., p. 216.

But with the grey area, we have the thing, without the word. And we really *do* have the thing; one of the ways in which capital develops is by invading ever new spheres of life—or even *creating* them, as in the parallel universe of finance—in which laws are inevitably incomplete, and behaviour can easily become equivocal. Equivocal: not illegal, but not quite right either. Think of a few years ago (or of today, for that matter): Was it illegal for banks to have a preposterous risk-to-asset ratio? No. Was it 'right', in any conceivable sense of the word? Also no. Or think of Enron: in the months that led to its bankruptcy, Kenneth Lay sold stock at a grossly overstated price, as he knew perfectly well; in the criminal case, the government did not charge him; in the civil case it did, because the standard of proof was lower.[3] The same act that *is* and *is not* prosecuted: this is almost baroque, in its play of light and shadow, but exemplary: the law itself, acknowledging the existence of the grey area. One does something because there is no explicit norm against it; but it doesn't feel right, and the fear of being held accountable instigates endless cover-up. Grey on grey: a dubious act, wrapped in equivocations. The initial 'substantive conduct may be somewhat ambiguous', a prosecutor put it a few years ago, 'but the obstructive conduct may be clear'.[4] The first move may remain forever undecidable; but what followed it—the 'lie', as Ibsen will call it—that, is unmistakable.

The initial act may be ambiguous . . . That's how things begin, in the grey area: an unplanned opportunity arises all by itself: a fortuitous fire; a partner suddenly ousted from the picture; anonymous rumours; a rival's lost papers that show up in the wrong place and time. Accidents. But accidents that happen so frequently,

---

3   See Kurt Eichenwald, 'Ex-Chief of Enron Pleads Not Guilty to 11 Felony Counts', *New York Times*, 9 July 2004.
4   Jonathan Glater, 'On Wall Street Today, a Break from the Past', *New York Times*, 4 May 2004.

and with such long-term effects, that they become the hidden foundation of existence. Unrepeatable as the initial event usually is, the lie endures for years, or even decades; it becomes 'life'. That's probably why there is no keyword, here: just as some banks are too big to fail, the grey area is too pervasive to be acknowledged; at most, a cascade of metaphors—'fog of financialization', 'opaque data', 'dark pools', 'shadow banking'—that reiterate the greyness without really explaining what it is. And the reason for this half-blindness is that the grey area casts too bleak a shadow on the value which is the bourgeoisie's justification in the face of the world: honesty. Honesty is for this class what honour had been for the aristocracy; etymologically, it even derives from honour—and there is in fact a historical *trait d'union* between them in the female 'chastity' (honour and honesty at once) so central in eighteenth-century bourgeois drama. Honesty tells the bourgeoisie apart from all other classes: the word of the merchant, as good as gold; transparency ('I can show my books to anyone'); morality (Mann's bankruptcy as 'shame, dishonour worse than death'). Even McCloskey's 600-page extravaganza on *Bourgeois Virtues*—which ascribes to the bourgeoisie courage, temperance, prudence, justice, faith, hope, love . . . —even there, the core of the argument has to do with honesty. Honesty, the theory goes, is *the* bourgeois virtue because it's so perfectly adapted to capitalism: market transactions require trust, honesty provides it, and the market rewards it. Honesty *works*. 'By doing evil we do badly'—we lose money—McCloskey concludes, 'and we do well by doing good.'

By doing evil we do badly . . . This is true neither in Ibsen's theatre, nor outside of it. Here is a contemporary of his, a German banker, describing the 'undecipherable machinations' of finance capital:

> Banking circles were and are dominated by a striking, very flexible morality. Certain kinds of manipulation, which no good *Bürger*

would in good conscience accept . . . are approved by these persons
as clever, as evidence of ingenuity. The contradiction between the
two moralities is quite irreconcilable.[5]

Machinations, manipulation, no good conscience, flexible morality . . . The grey area. Within it, an 'irreconcilable contradiction
between two moralities': words that echo almost verbatim Hegel's
idea of tragedy. And Ibsen is a playwright. Is this what draws him
to the grey area? The dramatic potential of a conflict between
honest *Bürger* and scheming financier?

2. 'Signs against signs'

The curtain rises, and the world is solid: rooms full of armchairs,
bookcases, pianos, sofas, desks, stoves; people move calmly, carefully, speaking in a low voice . . . Solid. Old bourgeois value: the
anchor against the fickleness of Fortune, so unstable atop her wheel
and her waves, blindfolded, garments blown by the winds . . . Look
at the banks built in Ibsen's time: columns, urns, balconies, spheres,
statues. Gravity. Then the action unfolds, and there is no business
that is stable and safe; no word that doesn't ring hollow. People are
worried. Sick. Dying. It's the first general crisis of European capitalism: the long depression of 1873–96, which Ibsen's twelve plays
(1877–99) follow almost year by year.

The crisis reveals the victims of the bourgeois century: *I vinti*: 'the
defeated', as Verga, one year after *Pillars*, entitled his plan for a
novelistic cycle, of which *Mastro-don Gesualdo* was the second (and,
as it turned out, last) volume. Krogstad, in *Dollhouse*; old Ekdal and
his son, in *The Wild Duck*; Brovik and his son, in *Solness*; Foldal and

---

5   The passage is quoted by Richard Tilly in 'Moral Standards and
Business Behaviour in Nineteenth-Century Germany and Britain', in Kocka and
Mitchell, *Bourgeois Society in Nineteenth-Century Europe*, pp. 190–1.

his daughter, but also Borkman and his son, in *John Gabriel Borkman*. Ekdal and son, Brovik and son . . . In this naturalist quarter-century, failure flows from one generation to the next, like syphilis. And there is no redemption, for Ibsen's defeated: they are the victims of capitalism, yes, but the *bourgeois* victims, made of exactly the same clay as their oppressors. Once the struggle is over, the loser is hired by the man who ruined him, and turned into a grotesque Harlequin, part parasite, part worker, confidante, flatterer . . . 'Why did you put us into this little box where everybody is wrong?' a student once asked about *The Wild Duck*. She was right, it's unbreathable.

No, the irreconcilable contradiction between honest and fraudulent bourgeois is not Ibsen's point. Someone *was* deceitful, in the prehistory of many plays, but his antagonist was often more stupid than honest—and anyway, he's neither honest nor an antagonist anymore. The only conflict between good *Bürger* and corrupt financier is in *Enemy of the People*: Ibsen's only mediocre play (which the Victorians loved). But in general, 'cleaning up' the bourgeoisie from its murky side is not Ibsen's project; it's Shaw's. Vivie Warren: who leaves her mother, her boyfriend, her money, everything, and—as the final stage direction has it—'goes at her work with a plunge'. When Nora does the same at the end of *Dollhouse*, she walks into the night, not to a nice white-collar job waiting for her.

What draws Ibsen to the grey area . . . Not the clash between a good and a bad bourgeoisie. Not an interest in the victims, for sure. The winners, maybe? Take old Werle, in *The Wild Duck*. He occupies the same structural position as Claudius in *Hamlet*, or Philip in *Don Carlos*: he is not the protagonist of the play (that's his son Gregers—just like Hamlet, or Carlos), but he is certainly the one with the greatest amount of power; he controls all the women on stage; buys people's complicity, or even affection; and he does all this without emphasis, in an almost subdued way. But in his past, there is something which isn't quite right. Many years earlier, after 'an incompetent survey',[6] his business partner Ekdal 'carried out illegal logging on state property'.[7] Ekdal was ruined; Werle survived, then prospered. As usual, the initial act is ambiguous: Was the logging truly the result of incompetence? Was it fraud? Did Ekdal act alone? Did Werle know—did he even 'lay a trap'[8] for Ekdal, as Gregers suggests? The play doesn't say. 'But the fact remains', says Werle, 'that [Ekdal] was convicted and I was acquitted.'[9] Yes, replies his son, 'I'm aware that no proof was found.' And Werle: 'Acquittal is acquittal.'

There is a 'mythology' by Roland Barthes, 'Racine is Racine', on the arrogance of tautology: this trope 'that resists thought', he writes, like 'a dog owner pulling the leash'. Pulling the leash is certainly in Werle's style, but that's not the point, here; acquittal is acquittal, that is to say: the outcome of a trial is a legal act—and legality is *not* the ethical justice Gregers demands: it's a formal notion, not a substantive one. Werle accepts this discrepancy between the two spheres, and so does Ibsen: as we have seen, in most of his plays a mix of immorality and legality is the precondition for bourgeois success. Other writers react differently. Take the masterpiece of bourgeois

---

6   As Sarah Allison explained to me, this 'incompetent survey' is a *very* grey area: the word 'uefterrettelig' is given as 'false, mistaken' in Brynildsen's *Norsk-Engelsk Ordbog* (Kristiania 1917) and translated as 'misleading' in Michael Meyer's 1980 edition of the play for Methuen; as 'inaccurate' in Christopher Hampton's (London 1980); 'fraudulent' in Dounia B. Christiani's (London 1980); 'disastrously false' in Brian Johnston's (Lyme, NH, 1996); and 'crooked' in Stephen Mulrine's (London 2006). The etymology of 'uefterrettelig'—a negative prefix 'u' + 'efter' ('after') + 'rettel' ('right') + a suffix 'ig' indicating that the word is an adjective—suggests something, or someone, which cannot be relied upon to be right: misleading, unreliable, or untrustworthy seem the best (but partial) equivalents for a word in which an objective untrustworthiness neither implies nor excludes the subjective intent to provide false information.

7   Ibsen, *Complete Major Prose Plays*, p. 405.
8   Ibid., p. 449.
9   Ibid., p. 405.

Britain. In *Middlemarch*, the banker Bulstrode begins his career by cheating a mother and child of their inheritance. A banker—and in fact, a devoutly *Christian* banker—in the grey area: a triumph of bourgeois ambiguity, made even more so by Eliot's use of free indirect style, which makes it almost impossible to find a standpoint from which to criticize Bulstrode:

> The profits made out of lost souls—where can the line be drawn at which they begin in human transactions? Was it not even God's way of saving His chosen? . . . Who would use money and position better than he meant to use them? Who could surpass him in self-abhorrence and exaltation of God's cause?[10]

A triumph of ambiguity—had Eliot stopped here. But she couldn't. A petty swindler, Raffles, knows the old story, and by a series of coincidences this 'incorporate past',[11] in Eliot's wonderfully Ibsenesque formulation, locates both Bulstrode and the child. While at Bulstrode's house to blackmail him, Raffles falls ill; Bulstrode calls a doctor, receives his orders, and follows them; later, though, he lets a housekeeper disregard them. He doesn't suggest it; he just lets it happen—and Raffles dies. 'It was impossible to prove that [Bulstrode] had done anything which hastened the departure of that man's soul',[12] the narrator says. 'Impossible to prove': 'no proof was found'. But we don't need proof; we have *seen* Bulstrode acquiesce in manslaughter. Grey has become black; dishonesty, has been forced to shed blood. 'Forced': because this is such an implausible narrative concatenation that it's hard to believe that someone with Eliot's profound intellectual respect for causality could have actually written it.

---

10   Eliot, *Middlemarch*, pp. 616, 619.
11   Ibid., p. 523.
12   Ibid., p. 717.

But write it she did; and when a great novelist contradicts her own
principles so openly, something important is usually at stake.
Probably, this: the idea of injustice protected by the cloak of legality—Bulstrode, guilty, wealthy, and unscathed by his early
actions—was for Eliot too bleak a view of her society. Mind you,
this *is* how capitalism works: expropriation and conquest, rewritten
as 'improvement' and 'civilization' ('who would use money and
position better . . .'). Past might, becomes present right. But
Victorian culture—even at its best: 'one of the few English books
written for grown-up people', as Woolf said of *Middlemarch*—
cannot accept the idea of a world dominated by *perfectly lawful
injustice*. The contradiction is unbearable: lawfulness must become
just, or injustice criminal: one way or the other, form and substance
must be realigned. If capitalism cannot always be morally good, it
must at least be always morally *legible*.

Not for Ibsen. In *Pillars of Society* there is a hint in that direction,
when Bernick lets his 'incorporate past' board a ship that he knows
will sink, like Bulstrode with the housekeeper. But then Ibsen
changes the ending, and never does anything like it again. He can
look at bourgeois ambiguity without having to resolve it; 'signs
against signs', as they say in *The Lady from the Sea* (1888): moral
signs saying one thing, and legal signs another.

Signs against signs. But, just as there is no real conflict between Ibsen's
victims and their oppressors, so that 'against' does not indicate an
opposition in the usual dramatic sense. It's more like a paradox:
lawful/injustice; unfair/legality: the adjective grates against the noun,
like chalk on a blackboard. Enormous discomfort, but no action. What
draws Ibsen to the grey area, I asked earlier . . . This: it reveals with
absolute clarity the *unresolved dissonance of bourgeois life*. Dissonance,
not conflict. Strident, unsettling—Hedda and her pistols—precisely
because there are no alternatives. *The Wild Duck*, writes the great
theorist of dissonance, does not solve the contradiction of bourgeois

morality, but articulates its insoluble nature.[13] This is where Ibsen's claustrophobia comes from; the box where everybody is wrong; the paralysis, to use a metaphor of the early Joyce, who was one of his great admirers. It's the same prison of other sworn enemies of the post-1848 order: Baudelaire, Flaubert, Manet, Machado, Mahler. All they do, is a critique of bourgeois life; all they see, is bourgeois life. *Hypocrite lecteur—mon semblable—mon frère!*

3. BOURGEOIS PROSE, CAPITALIST POETRY

So far, I have talked of what Ibsen's characters 'do' in the plays. Now I will turn to how they speak and, specifically, to how they use metaphors. (After all, the first five titles of the cycle—*Pillars*, *Dollhouse*, *Ghosts*, *An Enemy of the People*, *The Wild Duck*—are all metaphors.) Take *Pillars of Society*. Pillars: Bernick and his associates: exploiters that the metaphor turns into benefactors, in the semantic somersault which is typical of ideology. Then a second meaning emerges: the pillar is that (sham) 'moral credibility'[14] which saved Bernick from bankruptcy in the past, and which he now needs again to shield his investments. And then, in the last lines of the play, two more transformations occur: 'Another thing I have learned', says Bernick, is that 'it's you women who are the pillars of society'. And Lona: 'No, my dear—the spirit of truth and the spirit of freedom—*those* are the pillars of society.'[15]

One word; four different meanings. Here, the metaphor is flexible: it's like a pre-existing semantic sediment, which characters can bend to their different aims. Elsewhere, it's a more threatening sign of a world that refuses to die:

---

13   Theodor W. Adorno, *Problems of Moral Philosophy*, Palo Alto, CA, 2001 (1963), p. 161.
14   Ibsen, *Complete Major Prose Plays*, p. 78.
15   Ibid., p. 118.

I almost believe we *are* ghosts, all of us, Pastor. It's not only what
we inherit from our fathers and mothers that keeps on returning in
us. It's all kinds of old dead doctrines and opinions and beliefs, that
sort of thing. They aren't alive in us; but they hang on all the same,
and we can't get rid of them. I just have to pick up a newspaper, and
it's as if I could see the ghosts slipping between the lines. They must
be haunting our whole country, ghosts everywhere . . .[16]

They hang on, and we can't get rid of them. One of Ibsen's characters can:

Our home has been nothing but a playpen. I've been your doll-wife
here, just as at home I was Papa's doll-child. And in turn the children have been my dolls. I thought it was fun when you played with
me, just as they thought it fun when I played with them. That's been
our marriage, Torvald.[17]

Nothing but a playpen. It's a revelation for Nora. And what makes
the metaphor truly unforgettable is that it's the trigger for a wholly
different style. 'Doesn't it occur to you', she says, after changing
from her tarantella costume into everyday clothes, 'that this is the
first time we two . . . have ever talked seriously together?'[18]
Serious; that great bourgeois word; serious as mirthless, in this
bitter scene, but also as sober, concentrated, precise. Serious Nora
takes the idols of ethical discourse ('duty'; 'trust'; 'happiness';
'marriage'), and measures them against actual behaviour. She has
spent years waiting for a metaphor to come true: 'the most wonderful thing in the world' (or 'the greatest miracle', as it's also
translated); now the world, in the person of her husband, has forced

16   Ibid., p. 238.
17   Ibid., p. 191.
18   Ibid., p. 190.

her to become 'realistic'.[19] 'We are closing our accounts, Torvald.' How do you mean, he reacts; I don't understand you, What's that, What do you mean, What a thing to say . . . And of course it's not that he doesn't *understand* what she's saying: it's that for him language should never be so—serious. It should never be *prose*.

By now, readers of this book know that prose is its only true hero. It wasn't meant to be; it just happened, in trying to do justice to the achievements of bourgeois culture. Prose as *the* bourgeois style, in the broadest sense; a way of *being* in the world, not just of representing it. Prose as analysis, first of all; Hegel's 'unmistakable definiteness and clear intelligibility', or Weber's 'clarity'. Prose as, not inspiration—this absurdly unjustified gift from the gods—but work: hard, tentative ('Well, Torvald, that's not easy to say'), never perfect. And prose as rational polemic: Nora's emotions, fortified by thought. It is Ibsen's idea of freedom: a style that understands the delusions of metaphors, and leaves them behind. A woman who understands a man, and leaves him behind.

Nora's dispelling of lies at the end of *Dollhouse* is one of the great pages of bourgeois culture: on a par with Kant's words on the Enlightenment, or Mill's on liberty. How significant, that the moment should be so brief. From *The Wild Duck* on, metaphors multiply—it's the so-called 'symbolism' of the late Ibsen—and the prose of the early phase becomes unimaginable. And this time, metaphors are not the 'dead doctrines' of the past, or the illusions of an inexperienced young girl, but the creations of bourgeois activity itself. Two very similar passages, from Bernick and Borkman— two financial entrepreneurs, one at the beginning and one at the end of the cycle—will explain what I mean. This is Bernick, describing what a railway will bring to the economy:

---

19   Ibid., p. 206.

Think what a lift this will give the whole community! Just think of
the vast tracts of forest that'll be opened up! The rich lodes of ore to
mine! And the river, with one waterfall after another! The possibilities of industrial development are limitless![20]

Bernick is excited here: sentences are short, exclamatory, with those
'think!'s (think what a lift, think of the forest) that try to arouse his
listeners' imagination, while the plurals (tracts, lodes, waterfalls,
possibilities) multiply results in front of our eyes. It's a passionate
passage—but fundamentally descriptive. And here is Borkman:

Do you see those mountain ranges *there* . . . That's my deep, my
endless, inexhaustible kingdom! The wind works on me like the
breath of life. It comes to me like a greeting from captive spirits. I
can sense them, the buried millions. I feel the veins of metal, reaching their curving, branching, beckoning arms out to me. I saw them
before like living shadows—the night I stood in the bank vault with
a lantern in my hand. You wanted your freedom then—and I tried
to set you free. But I lacked the strength for it. Your treasures sank
back in the depths. *(His hands outstretched)* But I'll whisper to you
here in the silence of the night. I love you, lying there unconscious
in the depths and darkness! I love you, you riches straining to be
born—with all your shining aura of power and glory! I love you,
love you, love you![21]

Bernick's was a world of forests, mines, and waterfalls; Borkman's,
of spirits and shadows and love. Capitalism is de-materialized: the
'lodes of ore' have become kingdom, breath, life, death, aura, birth,
glory . . . Prose is overrun by tropes: a greeting from captive spirits, veins of metal beckoning, treasures sinking into the depths,
riches straining to be born . . . Metaphors—this is the longest

---

20   Ibid., p. 32.
21   Ibid., p. 1021.

metaphorical string in the entire cycle—no longer interpret the world; they obliterate it and then remake it, like the night fire which clears the way for masterbuilder Solness. Creative destruction: the grey area, become seductive. Typical of the entrepreneur, writes Sombart, is 'the poet's gift—the metaphorical gift—of calling up to the eyes of his audience ravishing pictures of realms of gold . . . he himself, with all the passionate intensity he is capable of, dreams the dream of the successful issue of his undertaking'.[22]

He dreams the dream . . . Dreams are not lies. But they aren't the truth, either. Speculation, writes one of its historians, 'retains something of its original philosophical meaning; namely, to reflect or theorize without a firm factual basis'.[23] Borkman speaks with the same 'prophetic style' that was typical of the director of the South Sea Company (one of the first bubbles of modern capitalism);[24] the grand—and blind—vision of the dying Faust; the faith 'that the golden age lies not behind, but ahead of mankind' that Gerschenkron saw as the 'strong medicine' needed for economic take-off:

> Can you see the smoke from the great steamers out on the fjord? No? I can . . . Hear that? Down by the river, the factories whirring! *My* factories! All the ones *I* would have built! Can you hear how they're going? It's the night shift. Night and day they are working.[25]

---

22 Sombart, *The Quintessence of Capitalism*, pp. 91–2. It's impossible to miss the erotic undercurrent of Sombart's words; not for nothing, he saw 'the classic type of the entrepreneur' in Faust, Goethe's most destructive—*and* creative—seducer. In Ibsen, too, the entrepreneur's metaphoric vision has an erotic component, as in Solness's hysterically chaste adultery with Hilda, or Borkman's repressed love for his wife's sister.

23 Edward Chancellor, *Devil Take the Hindmost: A History of Financial Speculation*, New York 1999, p. xii.

24 Ibid., p. 74.

25 Ibsen, *Complete Major Prose Plays*, p. 1020.

Visionary; despotic; destructive; *self*-destructive: this is Ibsen's entrepreneur. Borkman renounces love for gold, like Alberich in *The Ring*;
is jailed; imprisons himself at home for eight more years; and in the
rapture of his vision, marches into the ice to certain death. That's why
the entrepreneur is so important for the late Ibsen: he brings hubris
back into the world—and hence tragedy. He is the modern tyrant: in
1620, the title of *John Gabriel Borkman* would have been *The Banker's
Tragedy*. Solness's vertigo is the perfect sign of this state of affairs: the
body's desperate attempt to preserve itself from the deadly daring
demanded of a founder of kingdoms. But the spirit is too strong: he
will climb to the top of the house he has just built, challenge
God—'Hear me, Almighty . . . from now on, I'll build only what is
most beautiful in all this world'[26]—wave to the crowd below . . . and
fall. And this uncanny act of self-immolation is the right prelude to
my final question: So, what is Ibsen's verdict on the European bourgeoisie? What has this class brought into the world?

The answer lies in a wider arc of history than the 1880s and '90s; an
arc at the centre of which lies the great industrial transformation of
the nineteenth century. Before then, what the bourgeois wants is to
be left alone, as in the famous reply to Frederick the Great; or at
most, to be recognized and accepted. He is, if anything, too modest
in his ambitions; too narrow; Robinson Crusoe's father, or Wilhelm
Meister's. His aspiration is 'comfort': this almost medicinal notion,
halfway between work and rest: pleasure, as mere well-being.
Caught in a never-ending struggle against the vagaries of *Fortuna*,
this early bourgeois is orderly, careful, with the 'almost religious
respect for facts' of the first Buddenbrooks. He is a man of details.
He is the prose of capitalist history.

After industrialization, though more slowly than we used to think—
chronologically, all of Ibsen falls within Arno Mayer's 'persistence

---

26   Ibid., p. 856.

of the old regime'—the bourgeoisie becomes the dominant class; and one with the immense means of industry at its disposal. The realistic bourgeois is ousted by the creative destroyer; analytical prose, by world-transforming metaphors. Drama captures better than the novel this new phase, where the temporal axis shifts from the sober recording of the past—the double-entry bookkeeping of *Robinson* and *Meister*—to the bold shaping of the future which is typical of dramatic dialogue. In *Faust*, in the *Ring*, in late Ibsen, characters 'speculate', looking far into the time to come. Details are dwarfed by the imagination; the real, by the possible. It is the *poetry* of capitalist development.

The poetry of the possible . . . The great bourgeois virtue is honesty, I said earlier; but honesty is retrospective: you're honest if, in the past, you haven't done anything wrong. You can't be honest in the future tense—which is the tense of the entrepreneur. What is an 'honest' forecast of the price of oil, or of anything else for that matter, five years from now? Even if you *want* to be honest, you can't, because honesty needs firm facts, which 'speculating'—even in its most neutral sense—lacks. In the Enron story, for instance, a big step towards the great swindle was the adoption of so-called mark-to-market accounting: entering as actually existing earnings which are still in the future (at times, years in the future). The day the Securities and Exchange Commission authorized this 'speculation' on the value of assets, Jeff Skilling brought champagne to the office: accounting as 'professional scepticism', as the classical definition had it—and it sounds so much like the poetics of realism—was over. Now, accounting was vision. 'It wasn't a job—it was a mission . . . We were doing God's work.'[27] This was Skilling, after the indictment. Borkman: who can no longer tell the difference between conjecture, desire, dream, hallucination, and fraud pure and simple.

---

27 Bethany McLean and Peter Elkind, *The Smartest Guys in the Room: The Amazing Rise and Scandalous Fall of Enron*, London 2003, p. xxv.

What has the bourgeoisie brought into the world? This mad bifur-
cation between a much more rational and a much more *ir*-rational
rule over society. Two ideal-types—one before and one after
industrialization—made memorable by Weber and Schumpeter.
Coming from a country where capitalism arrived late, and encountered few obstacles, Ibsen had the opportunity—and the genius—to
compress a history of centuries into just twenty years. The realistic
bourgeois inhabits the early plays: Lona; Nora; perhaps Regina in
Ghosts. The realist as a woman: an odd choice, for the times (*Heart
of Darkness*: 'it's queer how out of touch with truth women are'). A
radical choice, too, in the spirit of Mill's *Subjection of Women*. But
also profoundly pessimistic about the scope of bourgeois 'realism':
imaginable within the intimate sphere—as the solvent of the nuclear
family and of its lies—but not in society at large. Nora's prose at the
end of *Dollhouse* echoes the writings of Wollstonecraft, Fuller,
Martineau:[28] but their public arguments are now locked inside a
living room (in Bergman's famous staging, a bedroom). What a
paradox, this drama that shocks the European public sphere, but
doesn't really *believe* in the public sphere. And then, once creative
destruction emerges, there are no Noras left, to counter Borkman's
and Solness's destructive metaphors; the opposite: Hilda, inciting
'*my* masterbuilder'[29] to his suicidal hallucination. The more indispensable realism is, the more unthinkable it becomes.

Remember the German banker, with his 'irreconcilable contradiction' between the good *Bürger* and the unscrupulous financier. Ibsen
of course knew the difference between them; and he was a playwright, looking for an objective collision on which to base his work.
Why not use this intra-bourgeois contradiction? It would have

---

28   The sources of Nora's speech have been identified by Joan Templeton;
see Alisa Solomon, *Re-Dressing the Canon: Essays on Theater and Gender*,
London/New York, p. 50.

29   Ibsen, *Complete Major Prose Plays*, p. 29.

made so much sense to do so; so much sense for Ibsen to be Shaw, instead of being Ibsen. But he did what he did, because the difference between those two bourgeois figures may perhaps be 'irreconcilable', but is not really a *contradiction*: the good *Bürger* will never have the strength to withstand the creative destroyer, and counter his will. Recognizing the impotence of bourgeois realism in the face of capitalist megalomania: here lies Ibsen's enduring lesson for the world of today.

ILLUSTRATION CREDITS

Introduction: Jan Steen, *The Burgher of Delft and his Daughter*, 1655. With permission from the Bridgeman Art Library.

Part 1: Frontispiece for *Robinson Crusoe*, author's own.

T. Pericoli, *Robinson e gli attrezzi*, 1984, India ink and watercolor on paper, 76x57 cm. With permission from Studio Percoli.

Part 2: Johannes Vermeer, *Woman in Blue Reading Letter*, 1663, oil on canvas, 47x39 cm. With permission from the Bridgeman Art Library.

Vermeer, *Love Letter*, 1669, oil on canvas, 44x38 cm. With permission from the Bridgeman Art Library.

Vermeer, *Officer and Laughing Girl*, 1657. Courtesy of the Frick Collection.

Gustave Caillebotte, *Study for a Paris Street, Rainy Day*, 1877, oil on canvas. With permission from the Bridgeman Art Library.

Part 3: Édouard Manet, *Olympia*, 1863, oil on canvas. With permission from the Bridgeman Art Library.

Jean Auguste Dominique Ingres, *Venus Anadyomene*, 1848, oil on canvas. With permission from the Bridgeman Art Library.

John Everett Millais, *A Knight Errant*, 1870. With permission from the Bridgeman Art Library.

Index